More Flies, Flowers, Fur & Feather

John Cawthorne

The Crowood Press

First published in 2004 by
The Crowood Press Ltd
Ramsbury, Marlborough
Wiltshire SN8 2HR

www.crowood.com

**British Library Cataloguing-in-
Publication Data**

A catalogue record for this book is available
from the British Library.

ISBN 1 86126 648 0

To
Wilf Skelton
Perfect Gentleman, Perfect Fisherman,
Perfect Friend

For
Anne, William, Carol and Peter

Many thanks to Carol, Jack Shardlow, Tom
Richardson, Stephen Moores, Sean Feeney,
Matthew Fletcher, Mary Jones, Wilf and Lilly
Skelton

Designed and edited by Focus Publishing,
Sevenoaks, Kent

Printed and bound in Malaysia by Times
Offset (M) Sdn Bhd

Acknowledgements

First, let me thank, as always, the splendid
river keepers of the Chatsworth Estate in
Derbyshire for their continued help and
support. River keeping must, at times, seem
like a thankless task when trying to maintain a
balance between the provision of sufficient
stockfish and the preservation of a healthy
natural population. The continuing fight
against poaching and pollution; the opening
up of bankside vegetation to provide
comfortable fishing with minimal disturbance
to wildlife; the provision of sufficient cover to
encourage invertebrate life in the form of
aquatic vegetation, rocks, gravel, and so on;
cleaning debris after winter floods and, of
course, performing a continual balancing act
to keep both skilled and unskilled fishermen
happy, are all part of their daily routine. It is
they who, in caring for the river or lake in their
charge, provide us with the pleasant
environment and conditions in which we love
to practise our 'gentle art'. So to all the river
keepers everywhere, and especially my
friends Stephen, Sean, Matthew and Tom,
may I thank you on behalf of fishermen
everywhere, for without you our sport would
not be so enjoyable.

I would also like to thank my old friend, Jack
Shardlow, who due to health problems has
now retired from fly-fishing. Without Jack's
encouragement years ago I would never have
taken up the sport that means so much to me
today, and for that and his companionship
over the years on our fishing forays I am
always in his debt.

Thanks also to Wilf Skelton, my present
fishing companion, whose infectious love of
the sport is passed on to everyone he comes
into contact with.

Contents

Foreword

This book is not only concerned with the pleasures of fly-fishing, but also with the whole experience of taking part in a pastime set in idyllic surroundings.

On the Chatsworth estate we are very fortunate to have two wonderful rivers, the Derwent and the Wye, which, although in close proximity to each other, are still full of contrasts. The Derwent, flowing through Chatsworth Park, is a full-bodied river, wide and clear with a good head of wild brown trout and rainbow trout, as well as grayling and a number of coarse fish. The Wye, in contrast, is gentler and much more ambling in its flow with wild rainbow trout, brown trout and grayling in the lower reaches. Besides supporting fish in quality and number, both rivers support a vast profusion of bird and animal life and waterside plants, and all these need to be taken into consideration in the management of our river systems. At the same time, we must not forget the need for public access, as wide as possible without causing detrimental effects to the environment we are trying to protect.

I sincerely hope that at Chatsworth we have been able to achieve the goals we have set for ourselves and have arrived at a balance that not only takes into account the natural environment but also the needs of the public in its use of this estate.

It is good to know that members of our fisheries also bear these things in mind and concern themselves both with the numbers of fish they catch and the enjoyment of the place itself.

In this sequel to *Flies, Flowers, Fur and Feather* John Cawthorne imparts his knowledge on fly-fishing and the pleasures of the whole river environment, illustrating both the artificials and the naturals on which they are based along with many of the flowers to be found whilst pursuing the 'gentle art'.

Devon

The Duke of Devonshire

Introduction

To blend into and become a part of one's environment is probably more important in fly-fishing, especially to the wandering river fly-fisherman, than in any other pastime. How often, when taking reasonable care with your approach, do you see the fish suddenly shoot off or sulk sullenly on the bottom? The fly-fisherman must be aware at all times that any sudden movements, heavy footfalls, obvious or clumsy casting of the rod, any disturbance of wildlife and the fish will be immediately alerted to his presence. If you watch a heron move with patience and stealth, striking only when completely confident of the result, you will see that while its total concentration is on fishing, it is also totally aware of its surroundings. As well as improving fishing skills, copying this awareness and involvement pays off in other ways as you will see birds and animals at much closer quarters if you are accepted as part of the environment. It will also bring you to a deeper and better understanding of the countryside, which we must care for and safeguard for future generations. No matter what the recreation or pastime, if it is carried out in harmony with and for the benefit of the countryside, then nature in all its diversity will be preserved.

If we are also to endear ourselves to a watching public then we need to be aware and respectful of the requirements of wildlife. Disturbing ground-nesting birds for instance, or trampling down rare plants does not show us in a good light and are easily avoided with a little knowledge and awareness. If problems with, say, water quality are observed then it is no use wandering off moaning that you have had a wasted day - report the problem to the river keeper, or failing that, the Environment Agency. Any complaints made about anglers reflect badly on us all, and in some cases such as leaving litter about or discarding line, these are justified. So if you see discarded line in a tree and you can remove it then do so. Be aware of the general public and don't just ignore them or regard them as an intrusion. A pleasant chat or a politely answered question all serve to improve the image of the angler. If children stop to watch, then show them your catch or the fly you are using and explain to them what it is for. In doing so you are perhaps helping to shape future fishermen as well as endearing yourself to their parents. Remember that when we fish there are also many other people enjoying different aspects of the countryside and that they have as much right to pursue their interest in pastimes such as walking, bird-watching and photography, as we do our fishing. Show them the respect you would expect in return.

Although we mostly fish, catch and release purely by choice, I have no qualms about killing or taking fish within limits. However, if you do kill a fish then do it the proper way and use a priest, the idea of smashing a fish's head on a stone or landing net handle does not present a proper picture and at times can seem barbaric. If any member of the public is watching who you feel may be sensitive to the idea of killing the fish, then be sensible and let it go. Barbed hooks can now no longer be justified and the damage to fish without them is greatly reduced. However, if you do find a damaged or diseased fish, the best thing to do is to kill it and remove it from the river system - it would be cruel to leave it to suffer unnecessarily.

In short, an awareness of and respect for the countryside will help to show the fisherman in a good light, and a little knowledge about the environment in which we fish can only strengthen our cause. In this, the second part of *Flies, Flowers, Fur and Feather* I hope to add to that knowledge.

The first part of my book dealt with upwinged and sedge flies. In this volume I shall deal with stoneflies and all other miscellaneous 'flies' on which trout are likely to feed. Together they are intended to give a comprehensive guide to natural flies and sufficient artificial flies to cover any eventuality when fishing. There are, of course, thousands of artificial patterns available and a choice had to be made as to which to include. As fly-fishing is not an exact science, it may be that you are not, after observing the natural, satisfied with any of the existing patterns. If that is the case then I hope that the illustrations will be of help in creating your own designs. Fly-fishing, unlike any other sport, has no universally fixed rules. Although there are times when I wonder if it would not be better if there were certain constraints, the main object of it all is to enjoy your days by the water.

I am sure some people will ask why I have bothered to include waterside plants and trees in the book as it certainly isn't necessary to have any knowledge of plant life to be a skilled fly-fisherman. However, plants are not only an essential part of the environment, they are also a total necessity to the life that depends upon them. Without plants there would be no insect life and without insect life there would be no feeding trout to cast a fly to. As such, I make no apology for including them.

As you will see, I have divided the book into three sections: the first covers the stoneflies; the second, any miscellaneous 'flies' that live part or all of their life cycle in water; and the third section covers all terrestrial 'flies'. The only exceptions are food items such as spiders and moths where some species are aquatic, others terrestrial. In these cases I have placed them under 'miscellaneous aquatic'. To round off the book, I have included several detailed drawings showing the metamorphic life cycles of the main insect forms and detailed drawings of other insects, beetles, moths and so on, where I felt it would be helpful in the design of artificials or identification of naturals.

PART 1

The Stoneflies

For the fly-fisherman, stoneflies have more or less always held third place in popularity, the first and second places being taken by the upwinged and sedge flies. Their importance, however, is relative to the type and nature of the waters you fish. In the more lowland type of river or lake, the stonefly is not a main food source as there are normally so many other food forms available in much greater numbers. However, in more stony rivers much better hatches occur and the stonefly is a more important part of the trout's diet. Partly due to this and their importance through the history of fly-fishing, they have not attracted as much attention as regards identification, or even with anglers' names. Large stonefly, medium stonefly, and small brown are names that cover several species that I am sure

would have been given more elaborate names if they had held the same status as the upwinged flies. This also applies to patterns, most of which are general type flies and are tied to cover a number of naturals. However, these should not be overlooked, and when fishing upland waters it is essential to carry at least a few of these in various sizes.

In this section I have, as far as possible, tried to link the artificials to the natural. In some of the species such as the yellow sally and the needle fly this is fairly easy. In others, for instance the larger stoneflies, they are so very similar that once you have made your choice of pattern it will cover several species, although some variations in nymphs are more obvious.

Early Brown Stonefly
Protonemura meyeri
(Plate 1)

This is one of the early season stoneflies, first appearing in March with the main flight period lasting into June. It is a species that prefers the faster-flowing rivers and streams with moss-covered stones. It is fairly widespread, and where found occurs in reasonably large numbers. Like most of the stoneflies it is of a uniform grey-brown appearance. The only point of any significance is a pale yellowish stripe on the head.

Nymph:
Size:	Up to 10mm
Colour:	Medium to dark grey-green, grey-brown
Remarks:	The wing buds are carried at an angle out from abdomen

Adult:
Size:	Female, up to 9mm. Male, up to 8mm
Colour:	Wings, grey-brown. Abdomen, pale mid-brown
Location:	Swifter-flowing streams and rivers with stony, moss-covered beds
Distribution:	Fairly widespread and common
Time of year:	March–June

Dressings
1. Moser Stonefly (Moser)

DRESSING

Hook length: 9mm
Thread: Brown
Abdomen: Brown poly yarn
Wing: Moser stonefly wing
Hackle: Furnace

2. Early Brown (Fogg)

DRESSING

Hook length: 9mm
Thread: Red-brown
Abdomen: Brown seal's fur thread showing through
Hackle: Half-palmered with grey coot feather

3. Early Brown Nymph (Leiser)

DRESSING

Hook length: 10mm
Thread: Tan
Tail: Tan goose biots
Abdomen: Medium brown dubbing
Thorax: As abdomen but slightly built up
Wingcases: Dark feather fibres in two folds
Legs: Brown hen

Lesser Trefoil
Trifolium dubium (**Plate 1**)
Pea family (*Leguminosae*)

Flower head: A yellow globe-shaped flower head up to 8mm across is formed by 10-25 florets

Leaves: Leaves are divided into three bluish-green, slightly toothed, oval leaflets

Flowering time: May–August

Height: Up to 30cm

Habit: Annual

Habitat: Grassy places, riverbanks and meadows

Distribution: Common, rarer in north and northwest Scotland

General: This, the commonest of the hop trefoils, was once grown as a fodder crop for cattle. It is referred to as a hop trefoil because of the similarity of the flower heads to true hops and trefoil alludes to the three leaflets. It is claimed that this was the shamrock plant that Saint Patrick used to explain the Holy Trinity and it is worn throughout Ireland on Saint Patrick's Day in March

Plate 1

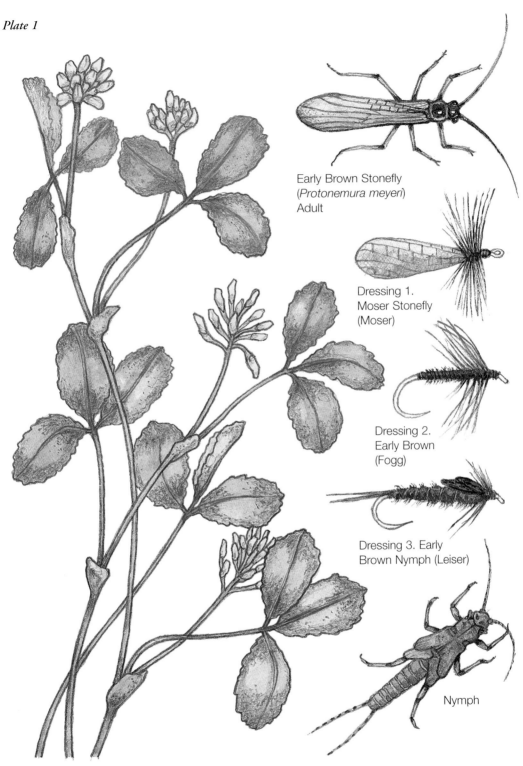

Early Brown Stonefly
(*Protonemura meyeri*)
Adult

Dressing 1.
Moser Stonefly
(Moser)

Dressing 2.
Early Brown
(Fogg)

Dressing 3. Early
Brown Nymph (Leiser)

Nymph

Lesser Trefoil (*Trifolium dubium*)

February Red Stonefly
Taeniopteryx nebulosa, *Brachyptera risi* (Plate 2)

Of the two species that share the same common name of February Red, *B. risi* is probably the more common and widely distributed. *T. nebulosa* is to be found in reasonably modest-flowing rivers with vegetation, whereas *B. risi* prefers the more normal stony river environment. The two species cover a flight period from February into July, *T. nebulosa* being the earlier. The wings are predominantly rich brown with two well-marked diagonal veins.

Nymph:
Size: Up to 12mm
Colour: Mostly brown with lighter markings
Remarks: Antennae and tails are longer than normal. Wing buds are carried at an angle away from abdomen

Adult:
Size: Female, up to 11mm. Male, up to 9mm
Colour: Wings, dark red-brown. Abdomen, grey-brown, last three segments red-brown
Location: *T. nebulosa*, modest-flowing rivers with vegetation. *B. risi*, faster-flowing rivers with stony beds
Distribution: Reasonably widespread and common
Time of year: *T. nebulosa*, February–April. *B. risi*, March–July

Dressings
1. Little Stonefly (Jardine)

DRESSING

Hook length: 11mm
Thread: Black
Abdomen: Dark brown fur (tail optional)
Wing: Dark grey-brown hen
Hackle: Dark brown

2. February Red (Fogg)

DRESSING

Hook length: 11mm
Thread: Dull orange
Abdomen: Claret and brown seal's fur sub
Hackle: Half-palmered woodcock

3. Small Stonefly Nymph (Price)

DRESSING

Hook length: 12mm
Thread: Black
Tail: Cock pheasant fibres
Abdomen: Brown latex or swannundaze
Thorax: Brown dubbing
Wingcases: Goose tied over thorax and two wing buds
Legs: Partridge fibres

Plate 2

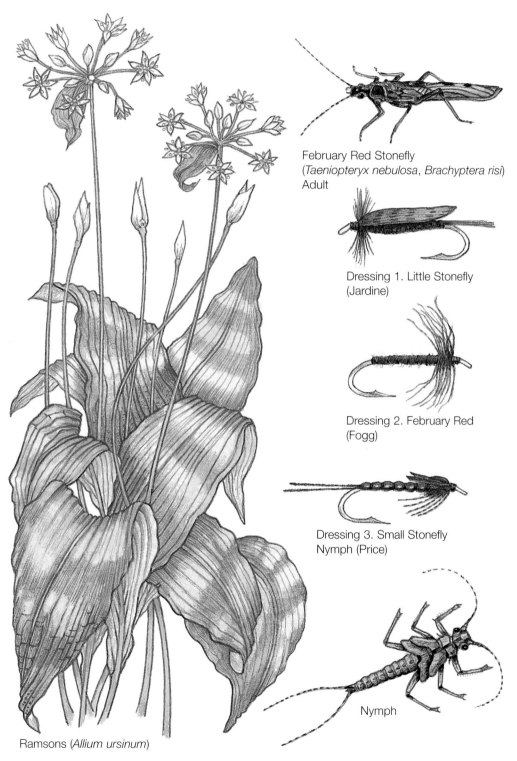

February Red Stonefly
(*Taeniopteryx nebulosa*, *Brachyptera risi*)
Adult

Dressing 1. Little Stonefly
(Jardine)

Dressing 2. February Red
(Fogg)

Dressing 3. Small Stonefly
Nymph (Price)

Nymph

Ramsons (*Allium ursinum*)

Ramsons
Bear's Garlic, Wild Garlic, Wood Garlic
Allium ursinum (Plate 2)
Lily family (*Liliaceae*)

Flower head: Terminal umbels of snowy white star-shaped flowers with six petals. Flower buds are enclosed in pale, papery sheaths

Leaves: Two or three elongated oval leaves with short stalks, bright green in colour

Flowering time: April–June

Height: Up to 40cm

Habit: Native perennial

Habitat: Woods, damp places, stream sides and shady places near water

Distribution: Common throughout

General: Wild garlic has a liking for moist, humus-rich soil and is a common sight in suitable habitats where it forms dense clumps that carpet the ground to the exclusion of all other plants. The leaves, which resemble lily of the valley, give off a highly pungent smell when crushed. They may be added to salads or used to flavour various dishes and sauces. If eaten by cattle a strong taste of garlic is given to the milk

Large Stonefly
Dinocras cephalotes
(Plate 3)

This species, along with *Perla bipunctata* is the largest of our stoneflies, attaining a length of up to 24mm. It is found in fast-flowing rivers with rocky beds. The chief identification feature is a solid brown-black segment to the thorax area. It is on the wing from late April into July.

Nymph:

Size:	Up to 28mm
Colour:	Dark grey-brown with paler segments, some markings to head and wing buds
Remarks:	Duller than *P. bipunctata* and not as strongly marked. Abdomen is flattened. Wing buds are held parallel to abdomen

Adult:

Size:	Female, up to 24mm. Male, up to 20mm
Colour:	Wings, brown well-marked veins. Abdomen, grey-yellow-brown
Location:	Fast-flowing rivers with rocky beds
Distribution:	Reasonably common and widespread
Time of year:	April–July

Dressings
1. Large Stonefly

DRESSING

Hook length: 20mm
Thread: Yellow
Tail and antennae: Goose biots
Abdomen: Dirty yellow dub
Rib: Yellow thread
Wing: Moser stonefly wing
Hackle: Red game cock

2. Stonefly Nymph (USA)

DRESSING

Hook length: 25mm
Thread: Yellow
Tail: Cock pheasant tail fibres
Abdomen: Dark hackle quill over lead strips
Thorax: Brown fur dub
Wingcase: Dark brown partridge
Legs: Brown partridge

2. Large Stonefly Nymph

DRESSING

Hook length: 25mm
Thread: Yellow
Tail and antennae: Brown goose biots
Abdomen: Rich brown dub
Rib: Gold wire
Thorax: As for abdomen
Wingcase: Turkey in three folds
Legs: Red game hen fibres

Sneezewort
Achillea ptarmica (Plate 3)
Daisy family (*Compositae*)

Flower head:	Branched terminal clusters of large daisy-like flower heads with three-lobed white petals and yellow stamens
Leaves:	Narrow, lance-shaped and finely toothed undivided leaves with no stalks
Flowering time:	July–August
Height:	Up to 60cm
Habit:	Perennial
Habitat:	Damp grassland, marshes and stream sides

Distribution:
General: Common throughout *Ptarmica*, from the Greek word *ptarmos* (sneezing), was first recorded in the sixteenth century by the herbalist, John Gerard. It was used as a kind of snuff, a powdered form being inhaled to induce sneezing and thereby cleanse the head. Another use was to hold a piece of root in the mouth to relieve the pain of toothache. The leaves, although rather bitter tasting, were occasionally added to salads

Plate 3

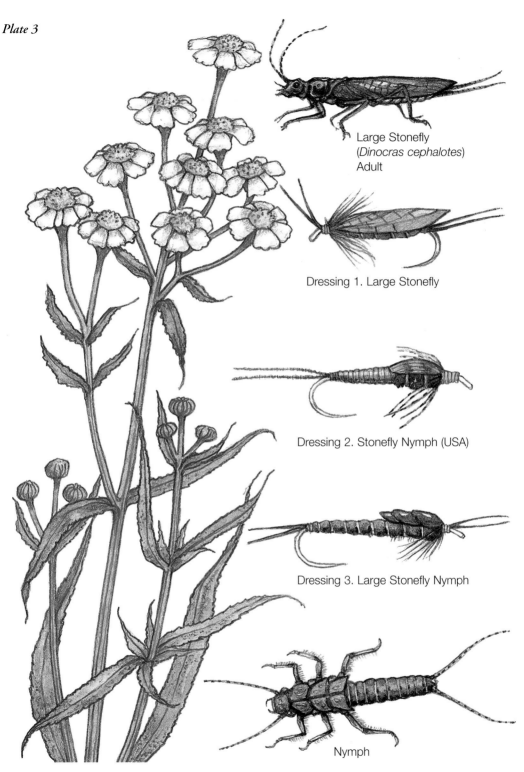

Large Stonefly
(*Dinocras cephalotes*)
Adult

Dressing 1. Large Stonefly

Dressing 2. Stonefly Nymph (USA)

Dressing 3. Large Stonefly Nymph

Nymph

Sneezewort (*Achillea ptarmica*)

Large Stonefly
Perla bipunctata (Plate 4)

This is one of the largest of the stoneflies and is found in the faster rivers and streams with rocky beds. It is reasonably numerous and widespread. The flight period stretches from April and well into June. The wings are brown with some darker markings, the abdomen is a pale brown-greyish-yellow and the thorax area has a pale yellow segment with dark brown-black markings.

Nymph:

Size:	Up to 26mm
Colour:	Very dark brown with bold yellowish markings
Remarks:	The nymph is flattened and wing buds are carried parallel to abdomen

Adult:

Size:	Female, up to 24mm. Male, up to 20mm
Colour:	Wings, brown with some darker markings. Abdomen, pale brown-greyish-yellow. Thorax, a pale yellow segment with some dark brown-black markings
Location:	Faster rivers and streams with stony beds
Distribution:	Reasonably widespread and fairly abundant
Time of year:	April–June

Dressings
1. Large Stonefly (Jansen)

DRESSING

Hook length: 22mm
Thread: Yellow
Tails and antennae: Stiff paintbrush bristle or sim
Abdomen: Trimmed muddler-style deer hair, dirty yellow
Thorax: Deer hair tied and pulled around hook in colour of abdomen
Wing: Coloured curtain material cut to shape
Hackle: Dark brown

2. Large Stonefly Creeper (Masters)

DRESSING

Hook length: 22mm
Thread: Black
Tails and antennae: 25lb bs mono
Abdomen: Brown antron
Rib: 10lb mono
Thorax: Brown antron
Wingcase: Brown raffene
Legs: Partridge body feather

3. Large Perla Nymph (Price)

DRESSING

Hook length: 24mm
Thread: Brown
Tails and antennae: Brown goose biots
Abdomen: Brown fur with some orange
Rib: Brown swannundaze or sim
Thorax: As abdomen
Wingcase: Three-stepped brown goose, varnished
Legs: Brown partridge

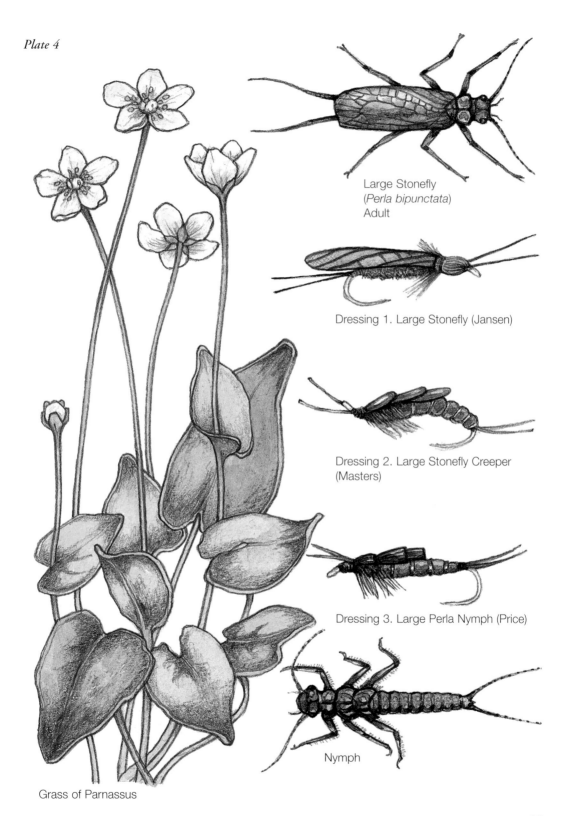

Plate 4

Large Stonefly
(*Perla bipunctata*)
Adult

Dressing 1. Large Stonefly (Jansen)

Dressing 2. Large Stonefly Creeper
(Masters)

Dressing 3. Large Perla Nymph (Price)

Nymph

Grass of Parnassus

19

Grass of Parnassus
(Plate 4)
Grass of Parnassus family
(*Parnassiaceae*)

Flower head:	Single white flowers held above the leaves on long stalks. Each flower is made up of five white petals with greenish veining and yellow stamens at the centre
Leaves:	Basal rosette of long-stalked, hairless, heart-shaped leaves and a single stalkless leaf just under halfway up each flower stalk
Flowering time:	July–October
Height:	Up to 30cm
Habit:	Perennial
Habitat:	Wet moorland, marshy ground, wet meadows
Distribution:	Most common in Scotland and northern England
General:	Despite its name, this plant is not actually a member of the grass family. It is named after Mount Parnassus in Greece, a mountain sacred to Apollo the god of music, where Dioscorides, a Greek physician, found it growing in the first century AD. The flowers, which attract insects for pollination, have a faint scent of honey. Other parts of the plant have medicinal properties – the leaves when boiled in wine or water may be used to dissolve kidney stones and treat liver disorders. Several species of the plant are cultivated as ornamentals

Large Stonefly
Perlodes microcephala
(Plate 5)

This is another species commonly called the large stonefly although it is not quite as large as *D. cephalotes* and *P. bipunctata*. For the most part it prefers the larger streams and rivers with rocky beds but can also be found on the southern chalk streams. The adult is greyish-yellow in the abdomen with brown marked wings.

Nymph:
Size:	Up to 23mm
Colour:	Dark brown with some contrasting markings
Remarks:	The nymph is moderately flattened, the wing buds are slightly prominent

Adult:
Size:	Female, up to 22mm. Male, up to 18mm
Colour:	Wings, brown with darker markings. Abdomen, greyish-yellow
Location:	Rivers and streams with rocky beds, stony lakes
Distribution:	Fairly common and widespread
Time of year:	April–June

Dressings
1. Adult Stone (Moser)

DRESSING

Hook length: 22mm
Thread: Brown
Tails and antennae: Goose biots
Abdomen: Dubbed and trimmed yellow deer hair
Thorax: As abdomen
Wing: Moser-shaped wing over head, thorax and body

2. Adult Stonefly (Roberts)

DRESSING

Hook length: 22mm
Thread: Brown
Abdomen: Yellow-brown poly dub palmered grizzle cock
Wing: Two brown feather slips over abdomen
Hackle: Dark red game cock

3. Stonefly Creeper (USA)

DRESSING

Hook length: 23mm
Thread: Yellow
Tail: Cock pheasant tail fibres
Abdomen: Stripped ginger hackle quill
Thorax: Amber fur dubbed
Wingcase: Barred Wood duck flank feathers over thorax
Legs: Brown partridge

Amphibious Bistort
Willow Grass
Polygonum amphibium
(Plate 5)
Dock family (*Polygonaceae*)

Flower head: Small pink flowers in a stout round spike on stems up to 1m long. The flowers, which are often in pairs, give off a scent of honey. They have no petals, the colouring coming from the sepals. There are five stamens and two styles

Leaves: Blunt, spear-shaped leaves floating on the surface at the end of long stalks. Leaves are hairless and have smooth margins

Flowering time: July–September

Height: Up to 1m

Habit: Perennial

Habitat: Canals, slow-moving rivers, pools and other wet places

Distribution: Widespread, common in southern and central England

General: *Polygonum* is from the Latin words *polys* (many) and *gong* (knee), referring to the plant's many jointed stems. *Bistorta* (twice twisted) is a reference to the contorted root system. Where it grows around the edges of bodies of water it forms large conspicuous clumps. The roots are completely submerged and only the leaves and flower heads show above the water. There is also a land form of willow grass, which has short, hairy-stemmed leaves and only grows to a height of 50cm

Plate 5

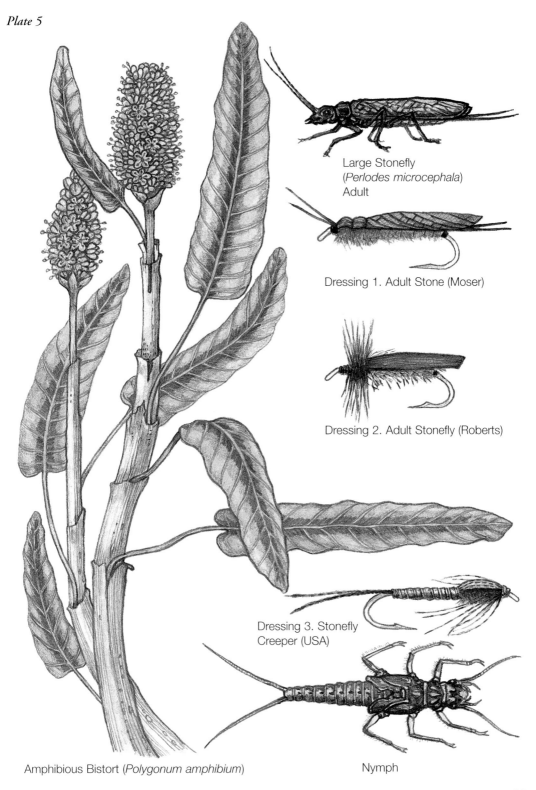

Large Stonefly
(*Perlodes microcephala*)
Adult

Dressing 1. Adult Stone (Moser)

Dressing 2. Adult Stonefly (Roberts)

Dressing 3. Stonefly
Creeper (USA)

Amphibious Bistort (*Polygonum amphibium*)

Nymph

Medium Stonefly
Diura bicaudata (Plate 6)

This species is to be found in the more
mountainous areas of Scotland, Wales and
the Lake District. It prefers fast-flowing
streams and rivers with stony beds, and also
some rocky lake shores. The body is browish-
yellow and the wings, which are brown with
some darker markings, are held rolled over
the upper abdomen. It is seen on the wing
from April to early July.

Nymph:
Size:	Up to 16mm
Colour:	Brownish-grey with yellow-olive markings
Remarks:	Wing buds carried only slightly at an angle from abdomen

Adult:
Size:	Female, up to 14mm. Male, up to 12mm
Colour:	Wings, brown with darker markings. Abdomen, brownish-yellow
Location:	Stony rivers and streams with a good flow, also some stony lake shores
Distribution:	Localized – Wales, Scotland and the Lake District
Time of year:	April–July

Dressings
1. Wonderwing Stonefly (Lively)

DRESSING

Hook length: 14mm
Thread: Orange
Abdomen: Dubbed fur rusty colour
Wing: Designed from dark red game hackle
laid flat over abdomen with fibres pulled back
and varnished
Hackle: Two red game hackles front and rear

2. Spanish Needle (Pritt)

DRESSING

Hook length: 14mm
Thread: Orange waxed thread
Abdomen: Tying thread
Hackle: Dark brown hen
Head: A few turns of peacock herl

3. Medium Stonefly Nymph

DRESSING

Hook length: 16mm
Thread: Brown
Tail and antennae: Cock pheasant tail fibres
and two paintbrush bristles, dark brown
Abdomen: Dark brown dubbing
Rib: Gold wire
Thorax: Hare's ear picked out
Wingcase: Brown turkey fibres
Legs: Brown partridge

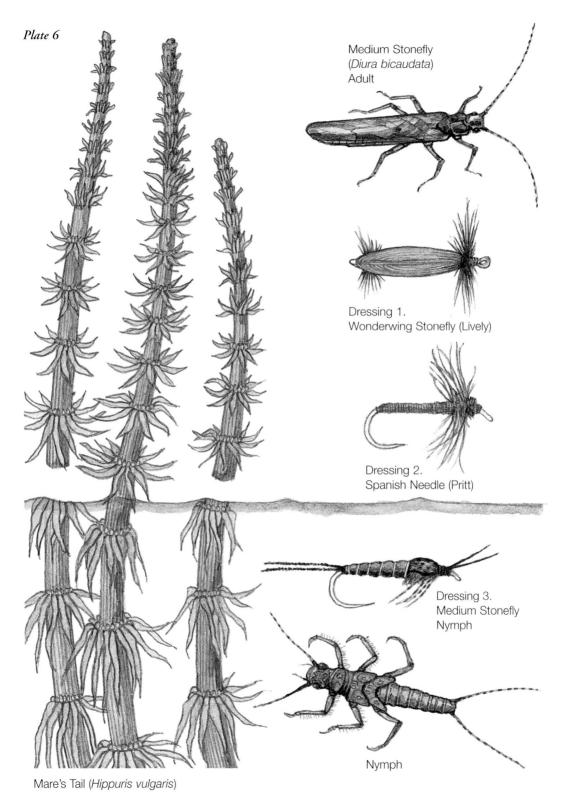

Plate 6

Medium Stonefly
(*Diura bicaudata*)
Adult

Dressing 1.
Wonderwing Stonefly (Lively)

Dressing 2.
Spanish Needle (Pritt)

Dressing 3.
Medium Stonefly
Nymph

Nymph

Mare's Tail (*Hippuris vulgaris*)

Mare's Tail
Hippuris vulgaris (Plate 6)
Mare's Tail family (*Hippuridaceae*)

Flower head:	Tiny green or pinkish flowers have neither petals nor sepals, consisting of just a single-celled ovary and stamen
Leaves:	Whorls of between six and twelve leaves on thick stems, dark green above the water but paler and more drooping beneath
Flowering time:	June–August
Height:	Up to 1m

Habit:	Perennial
Habitat:	Lakes, ponds, slow-running streams and rivers
Distribution:	Widespread, locally common
General:	*Hippuris* is from the Greek words *hippos* (horse) and *oura* (tail), and alludes to the appearance of the leaves on the stem. The only species in its family, this is an unusual plant in that it does not usually produce flowers but has masses of spores instead. Eskimos collect the young leaves and eat them as a vegetable

Needle Fly
Leuctra fusca: hippopus, inermis, nigra (Plate 7)

The needle fly is named for the way the wings are wrapped around the upper abdomen when at rest, giving the fly a very slim 'needle-like' appearance. The abdomen is dark brown as are the wings. It is a widespread species preferring stony rivers and streams, and still waters with stony margins. The flight period is reasonably late – from July into October. This is a very useful fly for the fisherman, particularly during the autumn.

Nymph:

Size:	Up to 11mm
Colour:	Greyish brown-yellow
Remarks:	Very slim shape, wing buds held in to abdomen

Adult:

Size:	Female, up to 9mm. Male, up to 7mm
Colour:	Wings, dark brown. Abdomen, dark brown
Location:	Stony rivers and streams, lake margins
Distribution:	Widespread and abundant
Time of year:	July–October

Dressings
1. Needle Fly

DRESSING

Hook length: 9mm
Thread: Dark brown
Antennae: Brown paintbrush bristles
Abdomen: Dirty yellow-brown dub
Rib: Dark brown thread
Wing: Feather slip flat over abdomen and slim
Hackle: Brown cock

2. Spanish Needle (Pritt)

DRESSING

Hook length: 9mm
Thread: Crimson
Abdomen: Thread dubbed sparsely with brown seal's fur sub
Hackle: Small starling feather or sim
Head: A few turns of peacock herl

3. Small Stonefly Nymph (Price)

DRESSING

Hook length: 11mm
Thread: Brown
Tail: Cock pheasant fibres
Abdomen: Brown latex or body glass
Thorax: Brown dub
Wingcase: Three goose biots, one over thorax, others tied in either side pointing over abdomen
Legs: Brown partridge

Marsh Thistle
Cirsium palustre (Plate 7)
Daisy family (*Compositae*)

Height:	Up to 2m
Habit:	Biennial
Habitat:	Fields, hedges, wet meadows, woods and other damp places
Distribution:	Common, especially north and west

Flower head: Masses of purple florets grow upwards from a rounded base of purple or greenish scale-like bracts. Carried at the top of stems or in leaf axils, they are 1–1.5cm across

Leaves: Narrow spear-shaped leaves that are deeply lobed and have long spines on the margins. They have hairy upper surfaces and are stalkless except for the basal leaves

Flowering time: July–September

General: This tall, spiny plant, which is so obviously a thistle, has a preference for moisture-retentive soil but avoids chalky habitats. Its appearance, especially its height, can be greatly affected by the conditions in which it is growing. The stem, which has narrow, spiny wings along it, contains a pith that is eaten by North American Indians

Plate 7

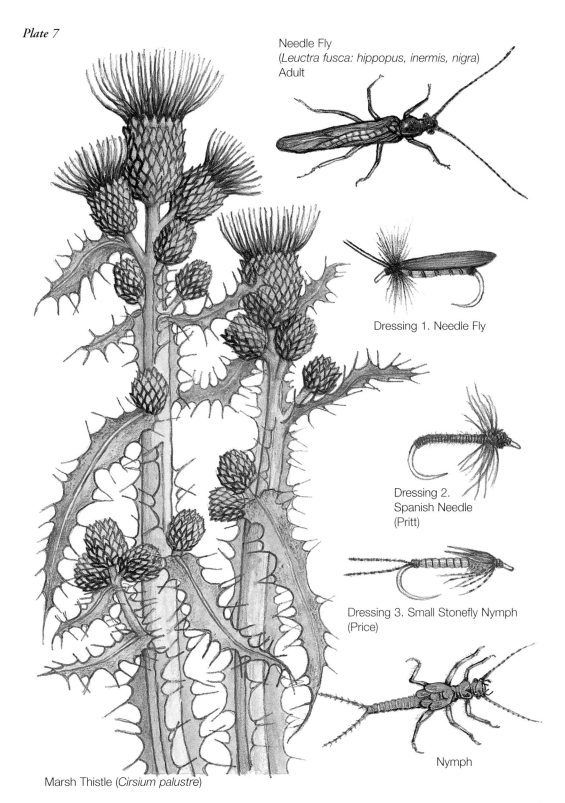

Needle Fly
(*Leuctra fusca: hippopus, inermis, nigra*)
Adult

Dressing 1. Needle Fly

Dressing 2.
Spanish Needle
(Pritt)

Dressing 3. Small Stonefly Nymph
(Price)

Nymph

Marsh Thistle (*Cirsium palustre*)

Small Brown Stonefly

Nemoura cinerea,
N. avicularis, N. cambrica;
Nemurella picteti (Plate 8)

There are several species known as the small brown and the differences between them are better left to the experts. The abdomen is dark brown and so are the wings. Some species prefer reasonably fast-flowing water with a stony bed, others, like *N. cinerea*, like slow or still water with good vegetation. The flight period is from April to early September. Due to the number of species bearing the same common name and the differences in habitat preference, the small brown can be said to be common and widespread.

Nymph:
Size: Up to 11mm
Colour: Olive-brown
Remarks: Very adaptable nymphs found in all kinds of waters including suitable ditches and very small streams. The wing buds are held at an angle from abdomen

Adult:
Size: Female, up to 9mm. Male, up to 7mm
Colour: Wings, dark brown. Abdomen, dark brown
Location: Mixed locations from still waters to stony streams, depending on species
Distribution: Common and widespread
Time of year: April–September

Dressings

1. Small Brown Stonefly

DRESSING

Hook length: 9mm
Thread: Rich brown
Abdomen: Dark olive-brown dub
Wing: Red game hackle tips tied slim and flat over abdomen
Hackle: Very dark brown cock

2. Wet Stonefly

DRESSING

Hook length: 11mm
Thread: Dark yellow, coated well with brown wax
Abdomen: Tying thread
Wing: Small dark brown feather
Hackle: Black hen

3. Small Brown Nymph

DRESSING

Hook length: 11mm
Tail and antennae: Cock pheasant tail herls
Abdomen: Olive-brown dub
Rib: Silver wire
Wingcase: Brown feather slips
Legs: Olive feather fibres

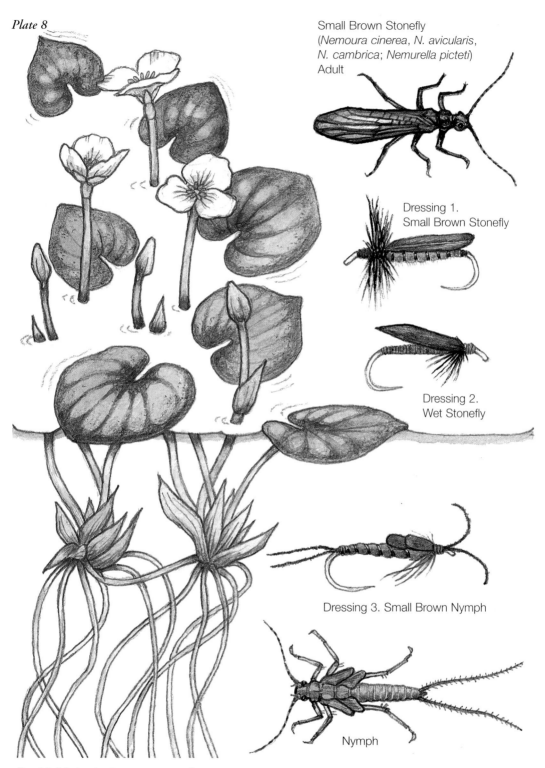

Plate 8

Small Brown Stonefly
(*Nemoura cinerea*, *N. avicularis*,
N. cambrica; *Nemurella picteti*)
Adult

Dressing 1.
Small Brown Stonefly

Dressing 2.
Wet Stonefly

Dressing 3. Small Brown Nymph

Nymph

Frogbit (*Hydrocharis morsus-ranae*)

Frogbit
Hydrocharis morsus-ranae
(Plate 8)
Frogbit family (*Hydrocharitaceae*)

Flower head:	White flowers held on long stalks above the water. Male and female flowers are separate, female flowers being solitary whilst male flowers are in clusters of two or three. Male flowers have three narrow sepals and petals with twelve stamens. Female flowers have the same and also an ovary with six styles
Leaves:	Floating rosette of long-stalked, kidney- to circular-shaped leaves, the lower surface often being tinged reddish-brown
Flowering time:	July–August
Height:	Up to 1m

Habit:	Perennial
Habitat:	Ponds, lakes, ditches
Distribution:	Throughout, except Scotland
General:	*Hydrocharis* is from the Greek words *hydro* (water) and *charis* (grace), and this graceful water plant is often grown for its beauty in ornamental ponds. Like many floating aquatic plants it has had to develop a means of passing through the harshness of winter. To do this it develops special winter buds that fall from the plant into the mud below. In spring, the bud develops into a new young plant that floats back up to the surface to continue its growth, rather like the phoenix rising from the ashes

Willow Fly
Leuctra geniculata (Plate 9)

Very similar to the needle fly in appearance, carrying its wings at rest wrapped over the upper part of the abdomen. The abdomen colour is a dark greyish-brown and the wings are dark brown. It is found in fast-flowing streams and rivers with stony beds, chalk streams and lake margins with stony shores. It is fairly abundant and widespread and is on the wing from late July into October.

Nymph:
Size: Up to 12mm
Colour: Yellow-grey-brown
Remarks: Very slim wing buds carried parallel to abdomen

Adult:
Size: Female, up to 10mm. Male, up to 8mm
Colour: Wings, dark brown. Abdomen, dark grey-brown
Location: Varied stony rivers, streams and lakes; occasionally chalk streams
Distribution: Reasonably widespread and abundant
Time of year: July–October

Dressings
1. Willow Fly

DRESSING

Hook length: 10mm
Thread: Dark brown
Abdomen: Brown and yellow dub
Rib: Tying thread
Wing: Feather slip tied flat over abdomen, dark brown
Hackle: Dark brown cock

2. Willow Fly Wet

DRESSING

Hook length: 10mm
Thread: Orange
Abdomen: Tying thread lightly dubbed with brown fur
Hackle: Brown partridge
Head: A few turns of peacock herl

3. Leuctra Nymph

DRESSING

Hook length: 12mm
Thread: Brown
Tail: Yellow-grey partridge
Abdomen: Yellow-brown dubbing
Rib: Tying thread
Thorax: Brown fur dubbing
Wingcase: Olive feather fibres in two steps
Legs: Yellow-grey partridge

Crack Willow
Salix fragilis (Plate 9)

Flower head: Small flowers clustered together to form male or female catkins. Male catkins are yellow and 2–5cm long. Female catkins are 6–10cm long and pale green in colour, maturing into white, woolly seedheads

Leaves: Narrow, often twisted, lance-shaped leaves taper to a fine point. Up to 18cm long, they are a rich, glossy green above and greyish-green below

Flowering time: Mid- to late spring

Height: Up to 24m

Habit: Native

Habitat: Riverbanks and watersides

Distribution: Common

General: Crack willows, which are either male or female trees, will, if grown to full height, develop long, upswept branches that become heavy and twisted with a rugged, deeply ridged bark. Older trees often grow slanted but they are more likely to be seen growing along riverbanks in a pollarded form where the branches are cut back to a level just above which cattle can reach. This results in the growth of straight young stems that are harvested to be used in the making of baskets and fencing. Timber from the tree is also used to make charcoal, which is very popular with artists as it gives a much less brittle product than other woods. The deep, penetrating roots make it a useful accomplice in the fight against erosion on riverbanks as they help to bind and hold together the soil. The Latin word *fragilis* (brittle) is a reference to the fact that twigs break off very easily at the base

Plate 9

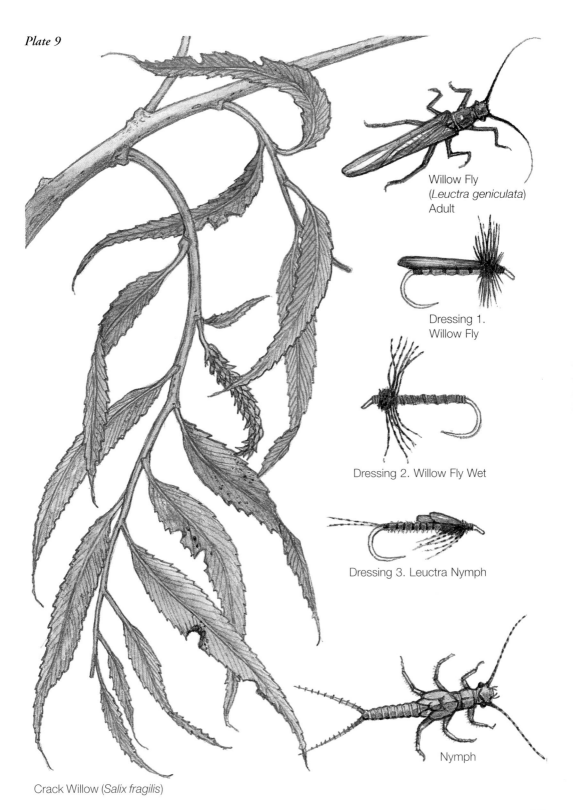

Willow Fly
(*Leuctra geniculata*)
Adult

Dressing 1.
Willow Fly

Dressing 2. Willow Fly Wet

Dressing 3. Leuctra Nymph

Nymph

Crack Willow (*Salix fragilis*)

Small Yellow Sally
Chloroperla torrentium
(Plate 10)

This, and the yellow sally, are the most obvious of the stoneflies in that they are both yellow in appearance. The difference between the two is in the size – as the name suggests this is a smaller fly. Although found throughout Britain it prefers, like most stoneflies, waters with stony beds. It is a common and abundant species where it occurs and a firm favourite with fishermen.

Nymph:
Size: Up to 10mm
Colour: Yellow with contrasting markings in brown
Remarks: The wing buds are rounded on the edges and carried parallel with the abdomen

Adult:
Size: Female, up to 8mm. Male, up to 6mm
Colour: Wings, yellow. Abdomen, brownish-yellow
Location: Waters with stony beds
Distribution: Widespread and abundant
Time of year: May–August

Dressings

1. Adult Stonefly (Veniard)

DRESSING

Hook length: 8mm
Thread: Yellow
Abdomen: Yellow seal's fur sub with a little hare's ear
Rib: Tying thread
Wing: Blue dun hackle tip flat over abdomen
Hackle: Grizzle cock

2. Roger's Stonefly (Woolley)

DRESSING

Hook length: 8mm
Thread: Olive
Abdomen: Olive-yellow seal's fur sub
Rib: Yellow rayon floss
Wing: Grizzle hackle tips
Hackle: Badger cock

3. Small Yellow Sally Nymph

DRESSING

Hook length: 10mm
Thread: Brown
Tails and antennae: Yellow goose
Abdomen: Yellow-brown fur dub
Rib: Copper wire
Wingcase: Brown feather fibres doubled
Legs: Yellow partridge

Plate 10

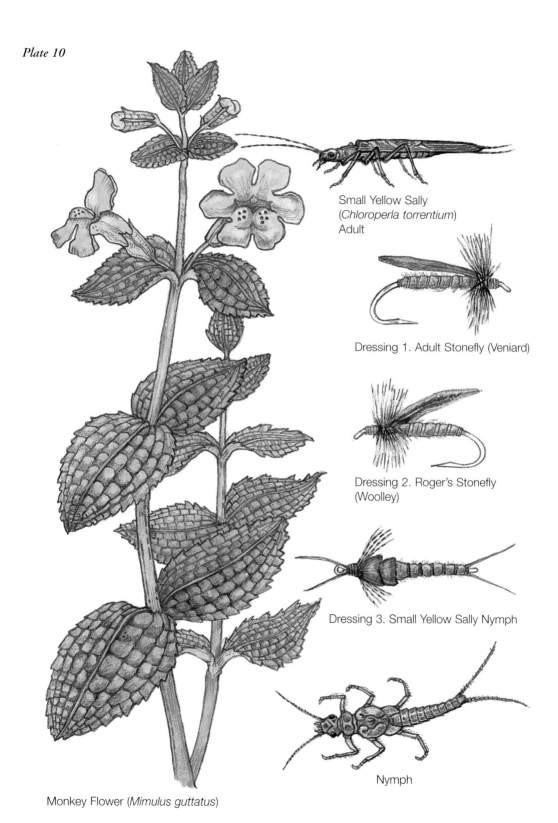

Small Yellow Sally
(*Chloroperla torrentium*)
Adult

Dressing 1. Adult Stonefly (Veniard)

Dressing 2. Roger's Stonefly
(Woolley)

Dressing 3. Small Yellow Sally Nymph

Nymph

Monkey Flower (*Mimulus guttatus*)

Monkey Flower
Mimulus guttatus (Plate 10)
Figwort family (*Scrophulariaceae*)

Flower head: Bright yellow, two-lipped flowers with red spots in the throat, up to 4.5cm across and carried on long stalks

Leaves: Opposite pairs of bright green oval leaves with toothed margins. Upper leaves are stalkless and clasp the stem

Flowering time: July–September

Height: Up to 50cm

Habit: Introduced perennial

Habitat: Stream and riversides, wet marshy places

Distribution: Common throughout, except East Anglia and Eire

General: This flower, which appears to mimic the face of a small monkey, was introduced from North America in the early nineteenth century. It quickly established itself in large numbers in Wales from where it spread to most of Britain, rapidly colonizing the waterways and canals where it can still be found in large colourful patches

Yellow Sally
Isoperla grammatica
(Plate 11)

Like the small yellow sally, this is fly of stony rivers and streams, and lake shores with a stony bottom. It can also be found on more typically lowland rivers, especially those with a limestone base. It appears towards the end of April but the larger hatches start in early June. Even on very hot, sunny days the female may be seen flying just above the water surface releasing her eggs.

Nymph:
Size:	Up to 14mm
Colour:	Contrasting yellow with brown markings
Remarks:	The nymph is slightly flattened, the wing buds are carried parallel to abdomen

Adult:
Size:	Female, up to 13mm. Male, up to 11mm
Colour:	Wings, yellow. Abdomen, brownish-yellow
Location:	Various rivers and streams, lake shores
Distribution:	Widespread and common
Time of year:	April–August

Dressings

1. Yellow Sally

DRESSING

Hook length: 13mm
Thread: Brown
Tails and antennae: Fine deer hair
Abdomen: Browish-yellow seal's fur sub
Rib: Gold wire
Wing: Yellow-brown Moser stonefly wing
Head: Yellow fly foam

2. Yellow Sally (Roberts)

DRESSING

Hook length: 13mm
Thread: Primrose
Tail: Ginger cock fibres
Abdomen: Yellow and brown seal's fur sub (5:1)
Rib: Primrose thread
Wing: Moser stonefly wing over abdomen
Hackle: Pale ginger cock

3. Yellow Sally Nymph (Price)

DRESSING

Hook length: 14mm
Thread: Yellow
Tails: Yellow-grey partridge
Abdomen: Yellow hare fur mixed with golden-stone haretron or sim
Rib: Gold wire
Thorax: Brown hare fur mixed with golden-brown haretron
Wingcase: Yellow goose in three steps
Legs: Yellow-grey partridge

Hemp Agrimony
Eupatorium cannabinum
(Plate 11)
Daisy family (*Compositae*)

Flower head: Tiny, muddy-pink, tubular florets forming dense flat-topped flower heads at the end of long, reddish, downy stems

Leaves: Lance-shaped, toothed leaves in opposite pairs and almost stalkless. The upper leaves are mostly three lobed

Flowering time: July–September

Height: To 1.5m

Habit: Native perennial

Habitat: Woodland, riverbanks, fens, marshes and other damp places

Distribution: Common in England and Wales, rarer elsewhere

General: Found in large colonies near watersides, this is the only member of its family to be found in Europe, the others being mainly native to North America. It is named after Eupator, King of Pontus, an area of Asia Minor. It was he who first discovered its use as an antidote to poison. It was also used medicinally to relieve jaundice and the common cold; and when applied as a poultice – sometimes mixed with pig's lard – to heal woulds

Plate 11

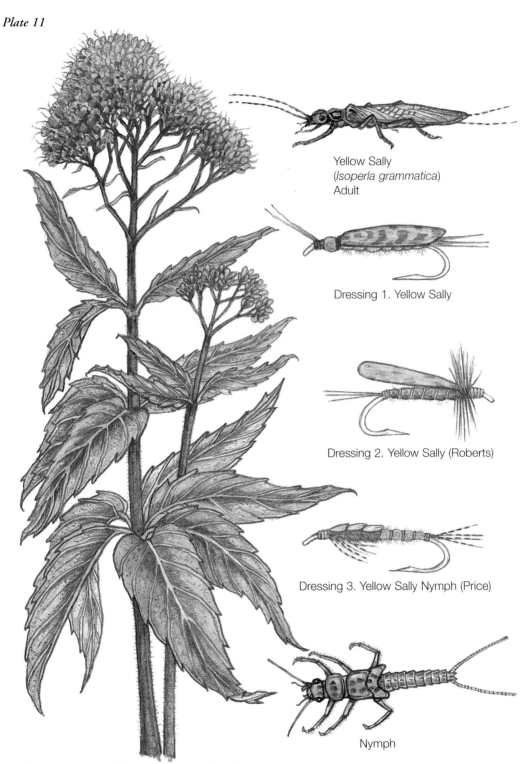

Yellow Sally
(*Isoperla grammatica*)
Adult

Dressing 1. Yellow Sally

Dressing 2. Yellow Sally (Roberts)

Dressing 3. Yellow Sally Nymph (Price)

Nymph

Hemp Agrimony (*Eupatorium cannabinum*)

PART 2

Miscellaneous 'Flies' (Aquatic)

('Flies' that live part or all of their life cycles in water)

Midges
Chironomids

This family of insects is amongst the most prolific and widespread of foods that are available to the fish. It is also one of the most difficult to identify and perhaps this is one of the reasons why, until recently, it has not been given much attention by the angler. However, midges are now becoming increasingly important to both the river angler and the stillwater fisherman for there will never be a day without some form of this creature being active on the water and so available to the trout.

Huge numbers of larvae and pupae, as well as adults are taken at different levels in the water system. Larvae, such as bloodworm, occur in millions on the lake bed when changing into pupae and can be taken at any level from bottom to mid-water, and especially whilst hanging in the surface film ready to hatch. As adults they will be taken readily from the surface whilst hatching off and when the female returns to lay her eggs.

Because of the lack of identified species, most of the information on this group of insects comes from the work of such people as John Goddard and Taff Price, who have given them names based mostly on the varied colours of the adults. It is still not possible to tie in colours of larvae or pupae to the appropriate adults, so in the following section I have tried to give a representative selection of the colours and patterns available. However, I think it can be reasonably assumed that the colour of the pupa will, in some ways, match the colour of the corresponding adult. The basic shape in all species is very similar in larvae, pupae and adults; the variation comes in colours and sizes. If you arrive at, or decide on a pattern that suits you, then it is simply a case of tying up the relevant colours and sizes to meet your needs.

Blae and Black Midge
Duck Fly
Chironomus anthracinus
(Plate 12)

Known as the duck fly in Ireland where it hatches in large quantities on the loughs, the blae and black midge can be seen on the wing at any time of day during the early part of the season. It must be remembered that whilst the adult is readily taken, just below the surface the rising pupae and emergers are also causing a great deal of interest. Although this particular species is mostly an early season fly, black 'midges' can be found at any time of year but some are of such small size as to be impossible to copy.

Adult:
Size:	Up to 7mm
Colour:	Wings, transparent white. Abdomen, grey-black
Time of day:	Throughout
Time of year:	Early season March–May

Dressings
1. Duck Fly (O'Reilly)

DRESSING

Hook length: 10mm sedge hook
Thread: Black
Abdomen: Black goose herls
Thorax: Black goose herls, some taken over thorax to give a pronounced hump effect
Wings: Two white-grey hackle tips
Legs/Hackle: Black hen

2. Knotted Midge

DRESSING

Hook length: 10mm
Thread: Black
Abdomen: Black thread
Hackle: Two small black cock hackles used to front and rear representing a pair of mating midges

3. F. Fly (Fratnik)

DRESSING

Hook length: 10mm
Thread: Black
Abdomen: Heron herl
Hackle: Grey *cul-de-canard* feather tied in over abdomen and trimmed to length

4. Rubber Band Bloodworm (Cove)

DRESSING

Hook length: 10mm
Thread: Red
Abdomen: Length of red rubber band tied on to hook and left to move freely. Rest of hook covered with red floss silk picked out

5. Suspender Midge Pupa (Goddard)

DRESSING

Hook length: 12mm curved hook
Thread: Black
Abdomen: Red-brown floss
Rib: Silver wire
Thorax: Peacock herl
A ball of ethafoam is enclosed in nylon tights material, this allows the 'pupae' to fish in the correct position

Wintercress
Yellow Rocket, St Barbar's Herb, Rocket Cress
Barbarea vulgaris (Plate 12)
Mustard family (*Cruciferae*)

Flower head:	Loose cluster of yellow flowers with four petals twice the length of the sepals in the shape of a cross
Leaves:	Shiny green leaves, the lower ones being deeply lobed whilst the upper ones are undivided and clasp the stem
Flowering time:	May–September
Height:	Up to 80cm
Habit:	Native perennial
Habitat:	Weedy areas, riverbanks and other wet places
Distribution:	Common in England, less so in Scotland
General:	The flower head, which is quite compact to begin with, lengthens as the fruit develops. The leaves, which are a rich source of vitamin C, resemble watercress and are sometimes eaten in salads. The French name for wintercress is *barbarée*, after Saint Barbara, the patron saint of miners and quarrymen – leaves from the plant were used to cover their wounds and assist healing

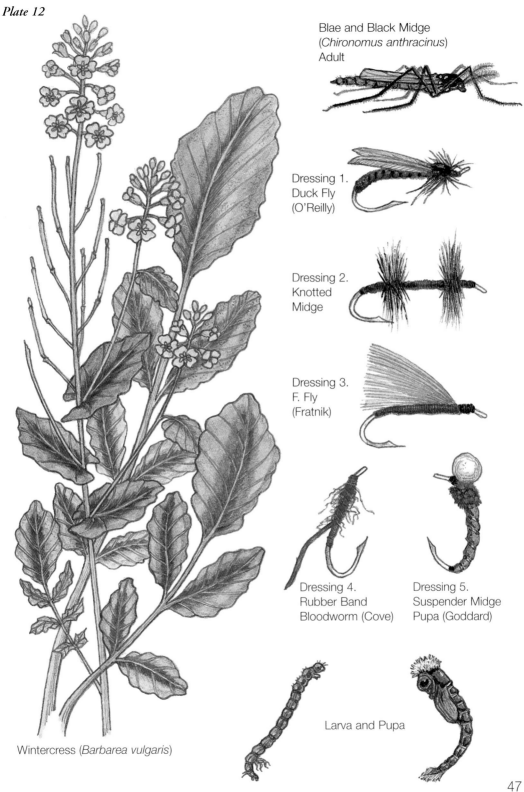

Plate 12

Blae and Black Midge
(*Chironomus anthracinus*)
Adult

Dressing 1.
Duck Fly
(O'Reilly)

Dressing 2.
Knotted
Midge

Dressing 3.
F. Fly
(Fratnik)

Dressing 4.
Rubber Band
Bloodworm (Cove)

Dressing 5.
Suspender Midge
Pupa (Goddard)

Larva and Pupa

Wintercress (*Barbarea vulgaris*)

47

Brown Midge
Chironomus riparius
(Plate 13)

This is a midge of slow-flowing and stagnant water. Because of the location, the larva will quite likely be of the 'bloodworm' type. The overall colour is gingery-brown with some yellow to the thorax area. The wings are clear with slight colouration to the leading edges.

Adult:
Size:	Up to 7mm
Colour:	Wings, transparent with slight brown tinge. Abdomen, gingery-brown
Time of day:	Throughout
Time of year:	Mid-summer

Dressings

1. Low-Riding Midge (Proper)

> **DRESSING**
>
> **Hook length:** 7mm
> **Thread:** Brown micro
> **Abdomen:** Thread thinly dubbed with ginger-brown fur
> **Wings:** Two hackle tips tied in slight 'V' over abdomen
> **Hackle:** Sparse tied pale brown cock bunched to either side of thorax then dubbed over and under with pale brown fur

2. Hatching Midge Pupa (Goddard)

> **DRESSING**
>
> **Hook length:** 12mm curved hook
> **Thread:** Brown
> **Tail:** White fluorescent wool strands
> **Abdomen:** Brown marabou or fine fluorescent wool
> **Rib:** Silver wire
> **Thorax:** Bronze peacock herl or fine brown dub
> **Breathing filaments:** Strands of white fluorescent wool

3. Bloodworm (Kendall)

> **DRESSING**
>
> **Hook length:** 12mm sedge hook
> **Thread:** Red
> **Tail:** Red marabou
> **Abdomen:** Red floss silk
> **Thorax:** Red and olive dub in equal parts

Plate 13

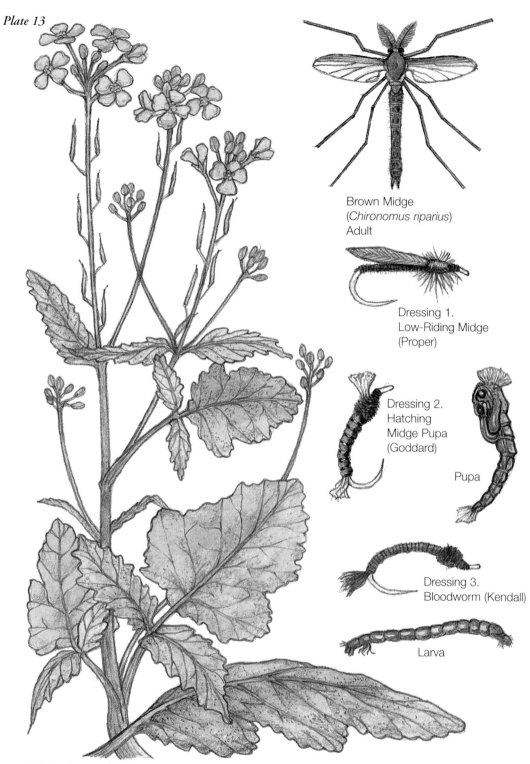

Brown Midge
(*Chironomus riparius*)
Adult

Dressing 1.
Low-Riding Midge
(Proper)

Dressing 2.
Hatching
Midge Pupa
(Goddard)

Pupa

Dressing 3.
Bloodworm (Kendall)

Larva

Black Mustard (*Brassica nigra*)

Black Mustard
Brassica nigra (Plate 13)
Cress family (*Cruciferae*)

Flower head: Four bright yellow petals, 8–10mm wide, in the shape of a cross

Leaves: Lower leaves are hairy with up to three lobes. Upper leaves are hairless, spear-shaped and stalked

Flowering time: May–September

Height: Up to 2m

Habit: Annual

Habitat: Waysides, waste places and riverbanks

Distribution: Common and widespread

General: Black mustard has been cultivated for hundreds of years for its oil, which is used both medicinally and in soap-making. In France the seeds are ground up and added to fermented grape juice to produce the familiar *moutarde* (mustard), the black seeds turning yellow when crushed. This ancient practice dates back to the thirteenth century. This used to be the case in Britain but now rape has taken its place. Mustard was used in a poultice to soothe aches and pains, and as a footbath to relieve colds and chest infections

Blagdon Green Midge
Endochironomus albipennis
(Plate 14)

This midge of the summer months hatches throughout the day. The thorax area is darker than the abdomen, which is bright green. It is seen in large numbers where it occurs and, as the name would suggest, is a common species on Blagdon Reservoir.

Adult:
Size:	Up to 6mm
Colour:	Wings, transparent. Abdomen, bright green. Thorax, brown
Time of day:	Throughout
Time of year:	Mostly June–August

Olive Midge
Chironomus plumosus
(Plate 14)

This morning and evening fly may be found throughout the summer months. The abdomen is olive-brown with creamy yellow segmentation, the thorax area is a grey-brown-olive. It is a reasonably common species found throughout Britain. It is said the pupa has similar colouration to the adult.

Adult:
Size:	Up to 7mm
Colour:	Olive-brown with distinct creamy yellow bands
Time of day:	Mostly early morning and evening
Time of year:	May–June, August–September

Large Green Midge
Chironomus plumosus
(Plate 14)

This fairly common midge is usually found hatching during the latter part of the day, especially on warm summer evenings in July and August. The abdomen is a dark olive-green and the thorax is brownish-green. The wings are transparent with a whitish tinge.

Adult:
Size:	Up to 8mm
Colour:	Wings, transparent with a whitish tinge. Abdomen, dark olive-green. Thorax, brownish

Dressings

1. Blagdon Green Midge (Williams)

DRESSING

Hook length: 9mm
Thread: Brown
Abdomen: Emerald green wool
Hackle: White cock

2. Olive Buzzer (Carnill)

DRESSING

Hook length: 10mm sedge hook
Thread: Olive
Abdomen: Olive herls
Thorax: Mole's fur dyed olive
Wings: Pale blue dun, rear facing and slightly spent
Hackle: Medium or pale olive hen hackle

3. Green Adult Midge (Walker)

DRESSING

Hook length: 9mm
Thread: Green
Abdomen: Green feather fibres
Rib: White hackle stalk
Thorax: Green feather fibres tied pronounced
Wings: Two small white hackle tips
Hackle: Pale green cock hackle

4. Midge Pupa (Roberts)

DRESSING

Hook length: 12mm
Thread: Green
Tail filaments: White fluorescent wool
Abdomen: Green floss silk
Rib: Silver wire
Thorax: Peacock herl
Head filaments: White fluorescent wool

5. Green Midge Larvae (Price)

DRESSING

Hook length: 12mm
Thread: Green
Tail: Green marabou
Abdomen: Green silk tied to emphasize segmentation
Rib: Fluorescent green silk
Thorax: Peacock herl

Monk's Hood
Helmet Flower, Turk's Cap, Soldier's Cap
Aconitum napellus (Plate 14)
Buttercup family (*Ranunculaceae*)

Flower head:	Deep blue or dark violet flowers with five petal-like sepals, the uppermost forming a helmet-shaped hood
Leaves:	Large alternate leaves deeply divided into five- or seven-toothed lobes
Flowering time:	June–September
Height:	Up to 1.5m
Habit:	Perennial
Habitat:	Damp woods, meadows and stream edges
Distribution:	Widespread
General:	Closely related to a number of garden species, this erect, almost hairless plant needs a damp soil in which to grow well. The helmet-shaped hood formed by the sepals make this plant very easy to identify. It is a source of aconitine, a drug used in the treatment of heart-related illnesses. Like all members of the buttercup family, monk's hood is a poisonous plant

Plate 14

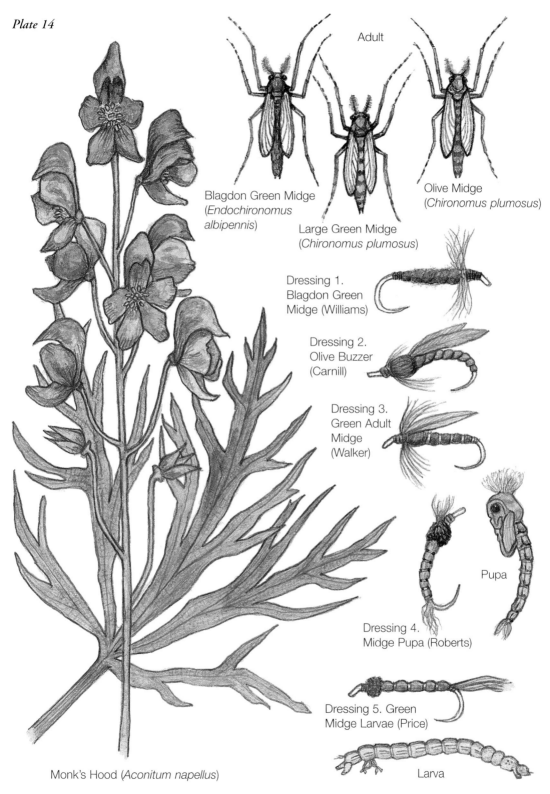

Adult

Blagdon Green Midge
(*Endochironomus albipennis*)

Large Green Midge
(*Chironomus plumosus*)

Olive Midge
(*Chironomus plumosus*)

Dressing 1.
Blagdon Green
Midge (Williams)

Dressing 2.
Olive Buzzer
(Carnill)

Dressing 3.
Green Adult
Midge
(Walker)

Pupa

Dressing 4.
Midge Pupa (Roberts)

Dressing 5. Green
Midge Larvae (Price)

Larva

Monk's Hood (*Aconitum napellus*)

Large Red Midge
Ginger Midge
Chironomus plumosus
(Plate 15)

This is one of the more colourful members of the larger species, being a bright red or gingery-orange. Some of the larger species hatch off in sparser numbers but nevertheless can still cause a good rise amongst waiting trout, especially to the rising pupa. The red midge hatches throughout the day, particularly in the warmer months of July and August.

Adult:
Size: Up to 8mm
Colour: Abdomen, dark orange-brown. Thorax and legs, gingery-orange
Time of day: Throughout
Time of year: Late June–September

Dressings
1. Red Adult Midge (Walker)

DRESSING

Hook length: 9mm
Thread: Red
Abdomen: Orange feather fibres
Rib: White hackle stalk
Thorax: Orange feather fibres
Wings: Two short white hackle tips
Hackle: Bright ginger cock

2. Palmered Midge

DRESSING

Hook length: 9mm
Thread: Red
Abdomen: Red wool body
Thorax: As abdomen
Hackle: Palmered blue dun cock

3. Red Midge

DRESSING

Hook length: 9mm
Thread: Red
Abdomen: Red seal's fur sub fine
Rib: Dark brown thread
Wing: White poly yarn tied over abdomen
Hackle: Short ginger-red cock

4. Hatching Buzzer Pupa (Collyer)

DRESSING

Hook length: 12mm sedge hook
Thread: Black
Abdomen: Red floss silk or feather fibres
Rib: Silver tinsel
Thorax: Fine deer hair trimmed to shape

5. Bloodworm (Bucknall)

DRESSING

Hook length: 14mm
Thread: Red
Tail: Red feather fibres tied with an up-curve
Abdomen: Red feather fibres
Rib: Oval silver
Thorax: Brown heron herl

Plate 15

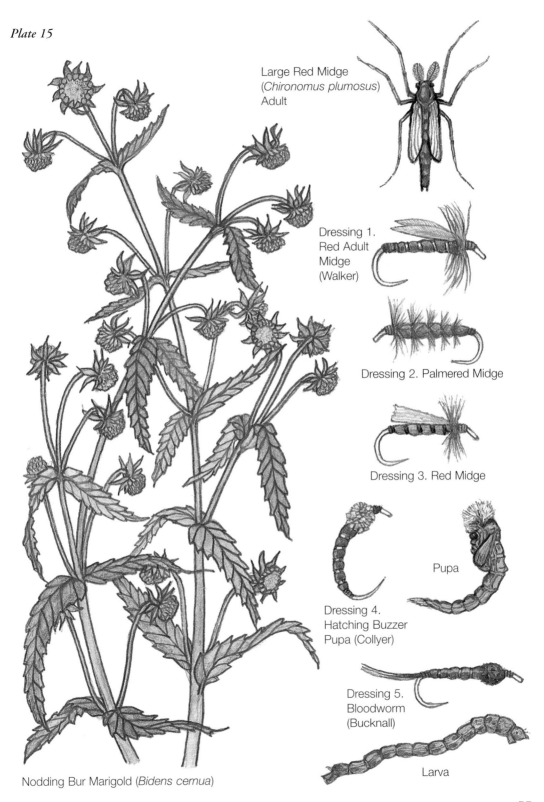

Large Red Midge
(*Chironomus plumosus*)
Adult

Dressing 1.
Red Adult
Midge
(Walker)

Dressing 2. Palmered Midge

Dressing 3. Red Midge

Pupa

Dressing 4.
Hatching Buzzer
Pupa (Collyer)

Dressing 5.
Bloodworm
(Bucknall)

Larva

Nodding Bur Marigold (*Bidens cernua*)

Nodding Bur Marigold
Bidens cernua (Plate 15)
Daisy family (*Compositae*)

Flower head: Drab yellow flowers in a flattish, disc-shaped head. An inner ring of yellow florets is surrounded by an outer ring of green leaflike bracts curling away from the flower, which is unscented

Leaves: Opposite pairs of stalkless, lance-shaped leaves with toothed margins

Flowering time: July–September

Height: Up to 60cm

Habit: Annual

Habitat: By still water, on banks of streams and ponds

Distribution: Locally common in southern England, rarer elsewhere

General: The Latin word *bidens* (two teeth) refers to the barbed spines (confusingly, the plant actually has four) on the seedheads that act as a means of distribution, attaching themselves to animals or clothing to ensure dispersal of the seed. This drab-looking plant with nodding flower heads is usually found on land that floods in winter but dries out in summer

Grey Boy
Orange Midge, Silver Midge
Chironomus plumosus
(Plate 16)

This is a very common species that can be found in most areas. Hatches occur throughout the day during May and June. The overall colour is a silvery-grey with orange-brown segmentation and orange patches to either side of the thorax area. The pupa mirrors the colours of the adult.

Adult:
Size:	Up to 8mm
Colour:	Wings, clear. Abdomen, silvery-grey with orange-brown segmentation. Thorax, grey with orange patches to either side
Time of day:	Throughout
Time of year:	May–June

Golden Dun Midge
Chironomus plumosus
(Plate 16)

As the name would suggest, the abdomen of this particular midge is golden-olive, the upper abdomen also carries some darker brown markings and the thorax area has darker markings to either side. This is another reasonably common and widespread species, mostly to be seen in early morning and towards dusk. It appears to favour the warmer months of summer.

Adult:
Size:	Up to 8mm
Colour:	Wings, transparent. Abdomen, golden-olive, some darker markings to top surface
Time of day:	Early morning and evening
Time of year:	July–early September

Yellow Striped Midge
Chironomus tentans
(Plate 16)

This is a species of midge that I believe was identified by Taff Price who also gave it its common name. I also believe in Germany it is called the twitching midge due to the twitching movements of the plumed antennae. The adult has a black abdomen with some yellow stripes on the thorax and the larva is red in colour. It is to be found in areas of reasonably still and stagnant water.

Adult:
Size:	Up to 7mm
Colour:	Abdomen, black. Thorax, black with yellow stripes

Dressings

1. Grey Midge

DRESSING
Hook length: 8mm
Thread: Orange-brown
Abdomen: Grey dubbing
Rib: Tying thread
Wings: Badger hackle tips
Hackle: Red game cock

2. Golden Dun Midge

DRESSING

Hook length: 8mm
Thread: Red-brown
Abdomen: Gingery-olive dubbing
Rib: Brown thread
Wings: Badger hackle tips
Hackle: Golden badger cock

3. Yellow Striped Midge

DRESSING

Hook length: 8mm
Thread: Yellow
Abdomen: Black dubbing
Rib: Tying thread
Wings: Badger hackle tips
Hackle: Yellow cock

4. Blagdon Buzzer (Bell)

DRESSING

Hook length: 12mm
Thread: Black
Abdomen: Black wool
Rib: Gold tinsel
Breathing filaments: A short tuft of white floss silk

5. Black Buzzer (Sibbons)

DRESSING

Hook length: 12mm
Thread: Black
Tail: White marabou tied short
Abdomen: Black floss, lead shot tied in at thorax
Rib: Copper wire
Breathing filaments: Short tuft of white deer hair

Soapwort
Fullers Herb, Bouncing Bet
Saponaria officinalis (Plate 16)
Pink family (*Caryophyllaceae*)

Flower head:	Pale pink, sometimes white flowers 25–35mm across in loose terminal clusters. Five unnotched petals are enclosed by five sepals that are joined to form a tube. Flowers may be double and are delicately scented
Leaves:	Opposite pairs of oval pointed leaves up to 10cm long, each with three or five prominent veins
Flowering time:	June–September
Height:	Up to 90cm
Habit:	Perennial
Habitat:	Waste land, woods, stream sides, hedgerows and roadsides
Distribution:	Common except in Scotland and northern England
General:	Soapwort was once widely grown as a cottage garden herb and it is probable that many plants now established in the wild were escapees from cultivation. *Saponaria* is from the Latin word *sapo* (soap). The green parts of the plant used to be boiled up in water to give a soapy liquid that was used for washing wool and other delicate fabrics – it is still occasionally used for washing antique fabrics and tapestries today. Soapwort was also used as a cure for gout and other skin disorders, and to produce a head on beer

Plate 16

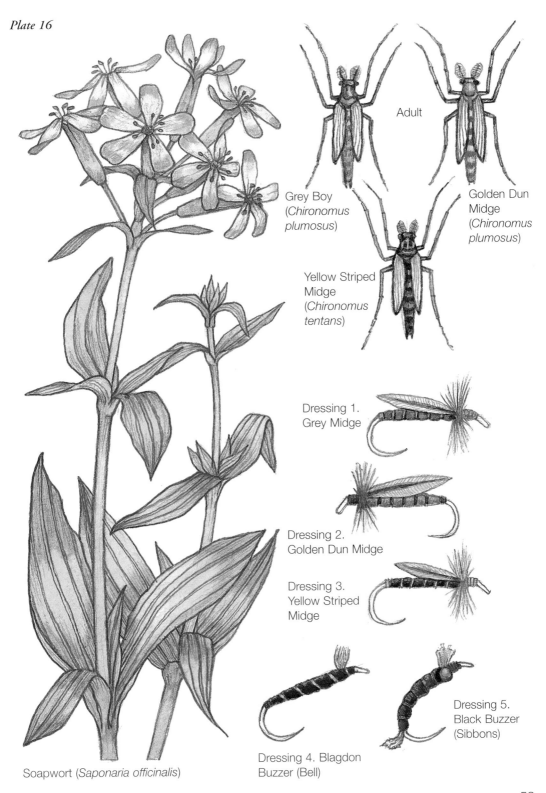

Grey Boy
(*Chironomus plumosus*)

Adult

Golden Dun Midge
(*Chironomus plumosus*)

Yellow Striped Midge
(*Chironomus tentans*)

Dressing 1.
Grey Midge

Dressing 2.
Golden Dun Midge

Dressing 3.
Yellow Striped Midge

Dressing 5.
Black Buzzer
(Sibbons)

Dressing 4. Blagdon Buzzer (Bell)

Soapwort (*Saponaria officinalis*)

Small Red Midge
Microtendipes pedullus
(Plate 17)

Very similar to the small brown in both size and colour. The abdomen is a rich red-brown and the wings are whitish tinged. It can be found on the wing throughout the day, particularly during late summer.

Adult:
Size:	Up to 6mm
Colour:	Wings, clear with whitish tinge. Abdomen, red-brown
Time of day:	Throughout
Time of year:	Late summer

Small Brown Midge
Glyptotendipes paripes
(Plate 17)

Although very similar to the small red midge, the body colour is more of a dark brown. Hatches are more prolific towards the evening, particularly during the hotter summer months.

Adult:
Size:	Up to 6mm
Colour:	Wings, greyish. Abdomen, dark brown
Time of day:	Towards evening
Time of year:	Midsummer

Small Black Midge
Polypedilum nubeculosus
(Plate 17)

A very common species often seen in large swarms on late summer evenings. They are so small and so large in numbers they become very difficult to imitate; almost in the 'caenis' class of fly. Trout will often be seen leisurely sipping them down one after another, especially when the hatch has been heavy. The abdomen is dark charcoal-black and the wings are greyish-white.

The pupae of these three species are very dark in colour and also very small.

Adult:
Size:	Up to 4mm
Colour:	Wings, greyish-white. Abdomen, charcoal-black
Time of day:	Mostly towards evening
Time of year:	Late summer

Plate 17

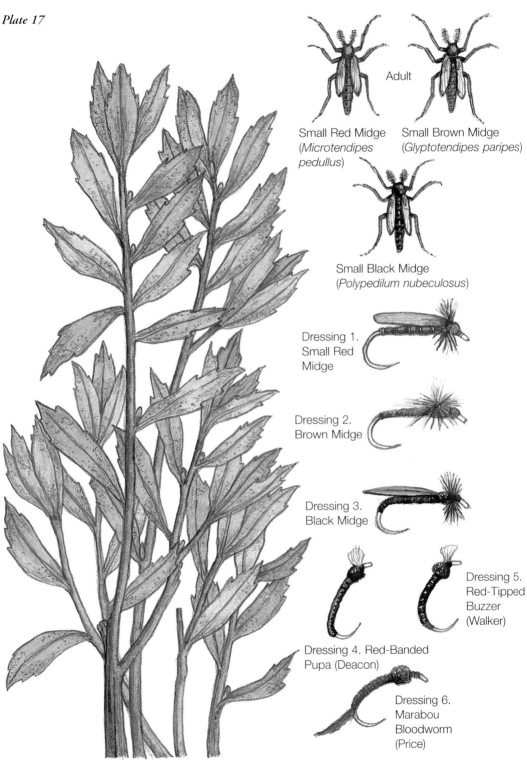

Adult

Small Red Midge
(*Microtendipes pedullus*)

Small Brown Midge
(*Glyptotendipes paripes*)

Small Black Midge
(*Polypedilum nubeculosus*)

Dressing 1. Small Red Midge

Dressing 2. Brown Midge

Dressing 3. Black Midge

Dressing 5. Red-Tipped Buzzer (Walker)

Dressing 4. Red-Banded Pupa (Deacon)

Dressing 6. Marabou Bloodworm (Price)

Bog Myrtle (*Myrica gale*)

Dressings

1. Small Red Midge

DRESSING

Hook length: 6mm
Thread: Dull red
Abdomen: Tying thread humped at thorax
Rib: Fine silver wire
Wing: Small white feather tips
Hackle: Red-brown cock, short

2. Brown Midge

DRESSING

Hook length: 6mm
Thread: Dark brown
Abdomen: Tying thread humped at thorax
Hackle: Red game, very short and tied parachute

3. Black Midge

DRESSING

Hook length: 4mm
Thread: Black
Abdomen: Tying thread
Wing: Tiny badger feather tips or fibres
Hackle: Very short black cock

4. Red-Banded Pupa (Deacon)

DRESSING

Hook length: 7mm
Thread: Black
Abdomen: Black silk with two turns of red tinsel near thorax, covered with fine nylon mono
Thorax: Fine black dub
Breathing filaments: Short tuft of white wool

5. Red-Tipped Buzzer (Walker)

DRESSING

Hook length: 8mm
Thread: Black
Abdomen: Fine black floss taken around bend of hook with small tip of red silk
Rib: Very fine silver wire
Thorax: Peacock herl
Breathing filaments: Fluorescent white wool

6. Marabou Bloodworm (Price)

DRESSING

Hook length: 8mm
Thread: Red
Tail: Short red marabou
Abdomen: Red silk
Thorax: Peacock herl

Bog Myrtle
Sweet Gale, Flea Wood
Myrica gale (Plate 17)
Myriceae

Flower head:	Flowers are in the form of short catkins, male and female being on different plants. Female catkins are smaller than the males and more orange in colour with a bristly stile
Leaves:	Grey-green stalkless leaves which are toothed toward the tip. Older leaves are hairy on the underside and have numerous yellow glands
Flowering time:	April–May
Height:	1–2m
Habit:	Native shrub

Habitat:	Bogs and wet heaths
Distribution:	Widespread where there are large areas of bogland
General:	This native shrub with its erect red stems often forms large fragrant clumps on the bogs and heaths where it grows. Its aromatic smell, which is evocative of eucalyptus, comes from a resinous substance secreted from the yellow glands on the undersides of the leaves. It was believed to have the power to repel fleas and as such was used in the Highlands to make flea-proof beds. It was also used to give beer its bitter taste before being replaced by hops

Mosquito
Culcidae (Plate 18)

Of the many species of mosquito, the most common are *C. culex* and *C. anopheles*. Large numbers of larvae are found in many locations ranging from tubs and water butts to ponds and lakes. All species are free-swimming. Pupae move in a wriggling motion, straightening and curling their bodies alternately. On reaching the surface, they curl up leaving their breathing horns breaking through the surface film. Some larvae hang at an angle to the surface but *C. anopheles* lies horizontally. Adult mosquitoes have slim bodies with long legs and a long proboscis that they use for extracting blood. The larvae grow up to about 10mm and are mostly green, grey or brown in colour. The pupae are similarly coloured but slightly smaller. The adults, which are dark brown and ginger with lighter colouring to the underside, also grow to about 10mm.

Adult:
Size:	Up to 10mm
Colour:	Dark brown and ginger with lighter underside
Time of day:	Towards evening
Time of year:	Warm summer evenings

Dressings
1. Adult Mosquito

DRESSING

Hook length: 10mm
Thread: Brown
Abdomen: Grey-brown dub
Rib: Brown thread
Wing: Honey hackle tips
Hackle: Ginger cock or Greenwell

2. Adult Mosquito (Price)

DRESSING

Hook length: 10mm
Thread: Black
Abdomen: Thinly dubbed grey polypropylene
Rib: Tying thread
Wing: Small grizzle hackles tied in spent
Hackle: Blue dun

3. Adult Mosquito

DRESSING

Hook length: 10mm
Thread: Brown
Abdomen: Grey dub
Rib: Tying thread
Wing: Grey polypropylene yarn tied over abdomen
Hackle: Brown cock

4. Mosquito Emerger

DRESSING

Hook length: 10mm
Thread: Black
Abdomen: Ginger-brown dub
Wing: Pale brown hackle tips
Hackle: Well-marked brown partridge

5. Mosquito Larva (Rosborough)

DRESSING

Hook length: 10mm
Thread: Grey
Tail: Barred guinea fowl feather
Abdomen: Grey yarn
Rib: Grey thread
Thorax: Grey dub
Breathing filaments: As tail

Plate 18

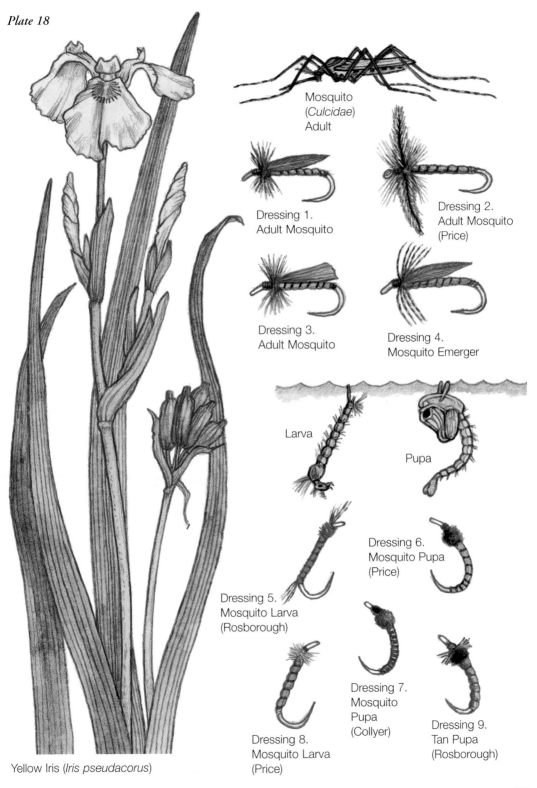

Mosquito
(*Culcidae*)
Adult

Dressing 1.
Adult Mosquito

Dressing 2.
Adult Mosquito
(Price)

Dressing 3.
Adult Mosquito

Dressing 4.
Mosquito Emerger

Larva

Pupa

Dressing 6.
Mosquito Pupa
(Price)

Dressing 5.
Mosquito Larva
(Rosborough)

Dressing 7.
Mosquito
Pupa
(Collyer)

Dressing 9.
Tan Pupa
(Rosborough)

Dressing 8.
Mosquito Larva
(Price)

Yellow Iris (*Iris pseudacorus*)

6. Mosquito Pupa (Price)

DRESSING

Hook length: 10mm
Thread: Grey
Abdomen: Grey silk taken around bend
Rib: Black thread
Thorax: Dubbed mole fur

7. Mosquito Pupa (Collyer)

DRESSING

Hook length: 10mm
Thread: Black
Abdomen: Stripped peacock-eye quill
Thorax: Muskrat or mole fur

8. Mosquito Larva (Price)

DRESSING

Hook length: 10mm
Thread: Grey
Abdomen: Grey silk
Rib: Black thread
Hackle: Clipped white cock

9. Tan Pupa (Rosborough)

DRESSING

Hook length: 10mm
Thread: Tan
Abdomen: Tan fuzzy yarn
Thorax: Black herl
Hackle: Clipped grizzle cock

Yellow Iris
Yellow Flag, Sword Flag
Iris pseudacorus (Plate 18)
Iris family (*Iradaceae*)

Flower head:	Bright yellow flowers up to 10cm wide appearing in clusters. Three large petals alternate with three smaller ones
Leaves:	Very long strap-like leaves with numerous fine parallel veins
Flowering time:	May–July
Height:	Up to 1.5m
Habit:	Perennial
Habitat:	Wet ground, shallow water, marshes and woods near rivers and streams
Distribution:	Common
General:	This familiar looking plant is a common sight near areas of water. Iris was the mythological Greek messenger who came to earth via a rainbow and it is this character after whom the plant is named. Iris flowers have long been a heraldic symbol, first adopted by Clovis, King of the Franks, in the fifth century. It is more familiar as part of the fleur-de-lis, as worn by Louis VII in the eleventh-century Crusades against the Saracens

Phantom Midge
Ghost Midge
Chaoborus (Plate 19)

The phantom midge, in its adult form, is similar in size and colour to other members of the midge family. The free-swimming larva, which has an air sac showing up as a black spot at either end of the body, lies horizontally in the water. The pupa, which is mostly found in still waters, marshes and ponds, has breathing horns and so tends to hang vertically in the water with its body outstretched. The larva is about 14mm in length, totally transparent and has a grey-greenish tinge. The pupa, which is pale grey-green with a bronze tinge to the thorax area, grows to about 12mm. The adult is usually a pale grey-brown and also about 12mm in length.

Dressings

1. Adult Phantom Midge (Goddard)

DRESSING

Hook length: 11mm
Thread: Orange
Abdomen: Grey condor herl
Rib: Olive-dyed PVC
Wing: White hackle tips tied semi-spent
Hackle: Honey cock tied back from eye

2. Adult Phantom Midge

DRESSING

Hook length: 11mm
Thread: Brown
Abdomen: Pale olive-grey dub
Rib: Tying thread
Wing: White poly yarn
Hackle: Tied in parachute around wing, pale olive cock

3. Phantom Pupa (Gathercole)

DRESSING

Hook length: 12mm
Thread: Brown
Tail: White feather fibres trimmed square
Abdomen: White silk covered in polythene
Rib: Silver wire
Thorax: Amber seal's fur sub
Wing buds: Pale brown feather fibres
Horns: As tail

4. Phantom Pupa (Collyer)

DRESSING

Hook length: 12mm
Thread: White
Abdomen: Flat silver tinsel
Rib: Oval silver tinsel, abdomen and rib then covered with polythene strip
Thorax: Few turns of peacock herl
Hackle: Short white hen

5. Phantom Larva (Russell)

DRESSING

Hook length: 12mm
Thread: Grey fluorescent floss
Abdomen: Tying floss taken round the bend tied slim, two black dots made to represent air sacs, then whole is clear varnished

6. Phantom Larva (Gathercole)

DRESSING

Hook length: 12mm
Thread: Brown
Abdomen: Silver lurex, small amount of tying thread left exposed at front and rear, abdomen then covered in clear polythene
Hackle: Very short white cock

7. Phantom Larva (Price)

DRESSING

Hook length: 12mm silver-coloured hook, slightly bent towards eye end
Thread: White
Tail: Small tail of white marabou
Abdomen: Two black dots painted on to silver hook, whole then covered with clear larva lace

Marsh Cudweed
Wayside Cudweed, Cottonweed
Gnaphalium uliginosum
(Plate 19)
Daisy family (*Compositae*)

Flower head:	Brownish-yellow, oval flower heads about 3–4mm across, grow from the leaf axils and at the ends of the stems. There is an inner disc of small florets surrounded by an outer circle of much larger ray florets
Leaves:	Narrow untoothed leaves, often broader above their mid-point and very hairy
Flowering time:	July–October
Height:	Up to 20cm
Habit:	Annual
Habitat:	Damp places, ditches and banks of streams
Distribution:	Common throughout
General:	This, the commonest of several cudweeds that may be found, is a great lover of acid soils. It is covered by masses of silver-grey hairs, hence its English name of 'cudweed' or 'cottonweed', and its scientific name which is Greek for wool

Plate 19

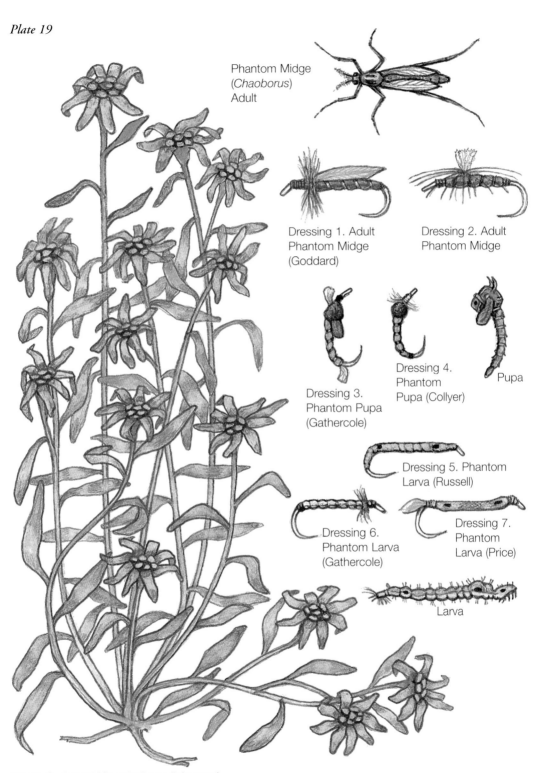

Phantom Midge
(*Chaoborus*)
Adult

Dressing 1. Adult
Phantom Midge
(Goddard)

Dressing 2. Adult
Phantom Midge

Dressing 3.
Phantom Pupa
(Gathercole)

Dressing 4.
Phantom
Pupa (Collyer)

Pupa

Dressing 5. Phantom
Larva (Russell)

Dressing 6.
Phantom Larva
(Gathercole)

Dressing 7.
Phantom
Larva (Price)

Larva

Marsh Cudweed (*Gnaphalium uliginosum*)

Alder Fly
Sialis fuliginosa, Lutaria
(Plate 20)

The alder fly is similar in size and shape to a sedge fly except that it has shiny wings whereas the sedge's wings are hairy. It is a fly known to all fishermen and is often seen in groups flying over and very close to the water surface. Despite this presence of adults in large numbers and the fact that artificials have been tied to represent them, it would seem that fish take very few. The larva, however, is a much different proposition for it grows quite large, presenting a sizeable snack for a feeding trout. It lives amongst silt and decaying matter on the riverbed or at the bottom of still waters, and when mature it crawls out of the water to pupate in soft soil at the water's edge. Adult insects hatch out from May onwards. The larva, which can grow up to 25mm long, has a single tail and long side gill filaments. It is an orange-brown colour with darker brown markings. The adult grows to about 14mm and has a grey-black abdomen and brown, shiny wings with darker veins.

Dressings
1. Adult Alder (Kingsley)

DRESSING

Hook length: 14mm
Thread: Black
Abdomen: Peacock herl dyed magenta
Wing: Brown hen
Hackle: Black shiny cock

2. Adult Larva (Jardine)

DRESSING

Hook length: 20mm
Thread: Dark brown
Tail: White marabou
Abdomen: Rust-coloured antron and hare's ear, white marabou tied in both sides of abdomen with gold wire rib
Thorax: Mix of brown and olive seal's fur sub
Thorax and back cover: Pheasant tail fibres
Legs: Brown partridge

Alder
European Alder
Alnus glutinosa (Plate 20)
Birch family (*Betulaceae*)

Flower head:	Tiny flowers are clustered together into catkins that are either male or female; both being present on the same tree. Male catkins are in clusters of between three and five. Originally 2–3cm long, they lengthen to 5cm when fully open and change colour from purplish in winter to dark yellowish tinged with

Plate 20

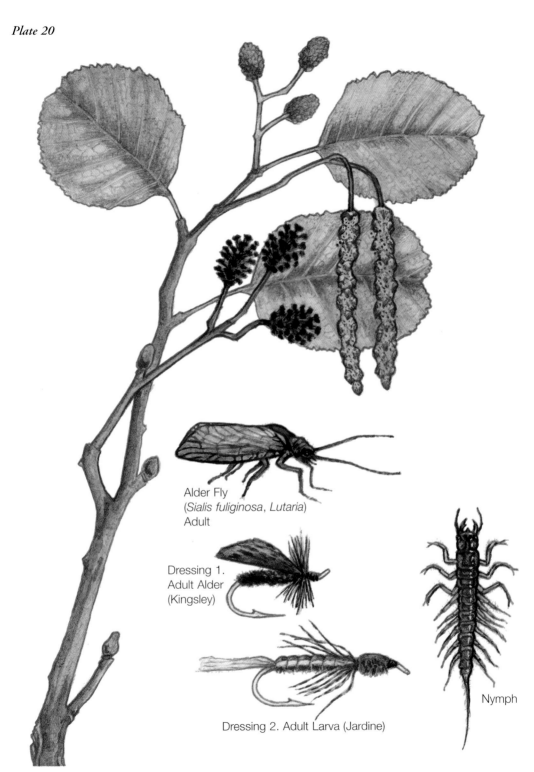

Alder Fly
(*Sialis fuliginosa*, *Lutaria*)
Adult

Dressing 1.
Adult Alder
(Kingsley)

Dressing 2. Adult Larva (Jardine)

Nymph

Alder (*Alnus glutinosa*)

crimson when fully ripe. Female catkins are in short, erect clusters that lengthen from 3cm to 5–6cm when fully open. They are dark red in colour

Leaves: Leaves are alternate and on short stalks, they have a slightly toothed apex and wavy, shallow-toothed edges. They are about 10cm long, dark green on the upper surface and paler beneath

Flowering time: Ripen March to late April

Height: Up to 22m

Habit: Native

Habitat: Stream and riverbanks, open waters and other wet places

Distribution: Common throughout

General: Alder is an attractive tree with shallowly fissured greyish-brown bark. Its roots are capable of fixing nitrogen and so it is a useful tree for enriching poor soils. Alder wood is easily carved and was once used in clog making; it is still used today for shoe soles, broom handles and waterside structures. When first cut, the timber is a creamy colour but this soon changes to a light reddish-brown, similar to the colour of blood. This gave rise to beliefs that evil spirits inhabited the tree. *Erlkonig* of German legends, for instance, actually means 'alder king' even though it is often translated as 'elf king'

Damselflies
Odonata (Plate 21)

Unlike the larger dragonfly, which is not very often seen in any numbers and is rarely, if ever, available to trout, the adult damselfly occurs at times and in places, especially when egg laying, that does make it available. When ready to lay her eggs, a female will first find a convenient stem down which she can crawl, abdomen first, to seek a suitable place to insert her eggs, which she does by means of her saw-like ovipositor. This involves being partly or often fully submerged underwater for some time, leaving her very vulnerable and accessible to the watchful trout. However, of much greater interest to the trout, and therefore of more importance to the fly designer, is the nymph stage in a damselfly's life. Nymphs are present in greater numbers and are far more readily available to the trout than the adults. Usually in shades of green or brown, the nymphs grow to 40mm in length. They are generally slender-bodied with three leaflike tails, pronounced wing buds and formidable jaws with which to grasp their prey. Adult damselflies may be found in a variety of colours but the most common are blue, red or green. They have a very slender, cylindrical abdomen and four wings which are uniform in size and shape. When at rest, the wings are held over the back but when fully open have a span of about 40mm. Damselflies may be seen on the wing in daylight hours between May and August but they do not have the same strong acrobatic quality of flight as dragonflies.

Dressings
1. Damselfly (Russell)

DRESSING

Hook length: 18mm
Thread: Blue
Abdomen: Extended beyond hook with blue feather fibres and dubbed blue seal's fur sub over blue fluorescent silk
Wing: Badger cock hackles tied in spent
Hackle: Dyed blue to match abdomen

2. Flyline Damsel (Tait)

DRESSING

Hook length: 12mm
Thread: Black
Abdomen: No. 7 floating fly line dyed blue and ribbed with tying thread extends beyond hook
Wing: Four black cock hackle tips tied on either side of thorax, semi-spent
Hackle: Black cock
Eyes: Two ethafoam balls in tights material tied in either side of thorax

3. Swimming Damsel Nymph (Price)

DRESSING

Hook length: 18mm, swimming nymph hook weighted to swim hook point upwards
Thread: Olive
Tail: Olive marabou
Abdomen: Medium olive, light brown and orange dubbing
Rib: Oval gold tinsel
Thorax: As abdomen
Wing case: Olive raffene over thorax
Legs: Olive partridge
Eyes: Two black beads

4. Damsel Nymph (Kendall)

DRESSING

Hook length: 18mm
Thread: Green
Tail: Three olive hackle points
Abdomen: Fine dubbing olive, dark olive, golden-olive, white (10:1:1:1)
Rib: Gold wire
Thorax: As for abdomen
Wing case: Olive feather fibres over thorax
Legs: Olive partridge fibres in four bunches, two either side of thorax
Eyes: Two brown beads or melted ends of brown mono

5. Damsel Nymph (Goddard)

DRESSING

Hook length: 18mm
Thread: Green
Tail: Three olive cock hackle tips
Abdomen: Medium olive seal's fur sub
Rib: Gold wire
Thorax: Olive-brown seal's fur sub
Wing case: Brown mallard feather fibres
Legs: Olive hen hackle fibres

Water Violet
Featherfoil
Hottonia palustris (Plate 21)
Primrose family (*Primulaceae*)

Flower head:	Pale lilac or pink flowers are carried in tiered whorls of between three and eight flowers on stems rising above the water surface. Each flower has a central yellow eye surrounded by five petals
Leaves:	Both submerged and floating leaves radiate from the stem in whorls of pale green, feathery segments
Flowering time:	May–July
Height:	Up to 50cm
Habit:	Perennial
Habitat:	Pools and ditches; and shallow, still or slow-moving water
Distribution:	Locally common in England and Wales
General:	Named after the Dutch botanist, Peter Hotton, the water violet is actually a member of the primrose family. It is an attractive plant with a large number of very delicate, finely divided leaves giving rise to its common name of 'featherfoil'. It is very popular in cultivation and is often found in garden ponds and ornamental lakes. In order to ensure its survival it has developed an interesting way of spreading itself over wider areas; small branches break away from the parent plant and are dispersed by the movement of the water to take root elsewhere

Plate 21

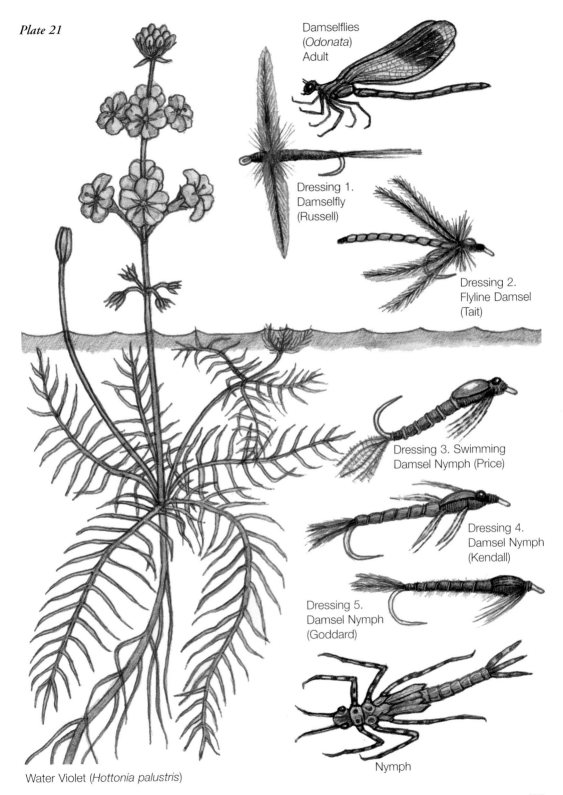

Damselflies
(_Odonata_)
Adult

Dressing 1.
Damselfly
(Russell)

Dressing 2.
Flyline Damsel
(Tait)

Dressing 3. Swimming
Damsel Nymph (Price)

Dressing 4.
Damsel Nymph
(Kendall)

Dressing 5.
Damsel Nymph
(Goddard)

Nymph

Water Violet (_Hottonia palustris_)

Dragonflies
(Plate 22)

Dragonflies in their adult form are rather solitary creatures and such strong fliers that they are of no interest whatsoever to the fly-fisherman. The nymphs, on the other hand, are often present in sufficiently high numbers to make them a worthwhile proposition from the fly-tiers point of view, and several well-known patterns exist to cover all the various colours that are likely to be found. The nymph is quite a formidable creature that is perfectly capable of taking small fish. It has very powerful jaws and an ability to move with quite a turn of speed; it accomplishes this by taking water in and then shooting it out at its rear end, giving it a kind of jet propulsion. As the nymphs spend a lot of time amongst the weeds, stones and sediment at the bottom, they are usually dirty green or brown in colour in order to blend in. Adults can attain a wingspan of up to 10cm; and the nymph of the emperor dragonfly can be up to 55mm long.

Dressings

1. Olive Dragonfly Nymph

DRESSING

Hook length: 22mm
Thread: Dark green
Tail: Two brown goose biots
Abdomen: Olive dubbed body tied fat
Rib: Copper wire
Thorax: Dark olive dubbing
Wing case: Mottled brown turkey
Eyes: Two red beads

2. Dubbing-Wick Dragonfly Nymph (Price)

DRESSING

Hook length: 22mm
Thread: Black
Tail: Two goose biots
Abdomen: Dubbing wicks of different colours twisted together in shades of olive, green and brown
Legs: Cock pheasant fibres
Head: As abdomen
Eyes: Bead or dumb-bell eyes

3. Dragonfly Nymph (Hopper)

DRESSING

Hook length: 22mm
Thread: Black
Tail: Olive goose biots
Abdomen: Olive-green seal's fur sub
Rib: Oval silver tinsel
Thorax: Peacock herl
Legs: Olive partridge

4. Dragonfly Nymph (Aulti)

DRESSING

Hook length: 22mm
Thread: Brown
Abdomen: Brown and grey marabou dub
Thorax: As abdomen
Wing case: Cock pheasant fibres
Legs: Cock pheasant fibres
Eyes: Two beads or burnt mono

Plate 22

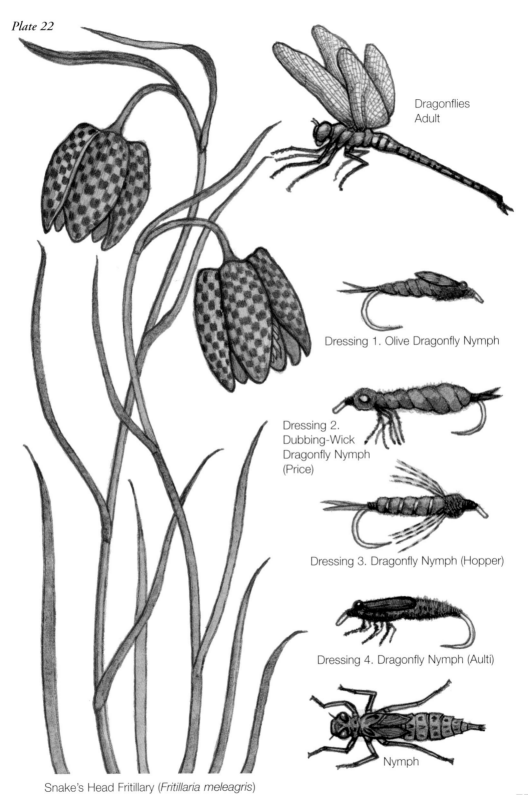

Dragonflies
Adult

Dressing 1. Olive Dragonfly Nymph

Dressing 2.
Dubbing-Wick
Dragonfly Nymph
(Price)

Dressing 3. Dragonfly Nymph (Hopper)

Dressing 4. Dragonfly Nymph (Aulti)

Nymph

Snake's Head Fritillary (*Fritillaria meleagris*)

77

Snake's Head Fritillary
Guinea-Hen Flower,
Chequered Lily
Fritillaria meleagris (**Plate 22**)
Lily family (*Liliaceae*)

Flower head: Single lantern-shaped flowers chequered in light and dark purple squares with a drooping habit

Leaves: Between three and six narrow leaves, which are blue-green in colour and taper towards the tip, decreasing in size towards the top of the stem

Flowering time: April–May

Height: Up to 40cm

Habit: Perennial

Habitat: Damp meadows and pastures

Distribution: Mostly southern and central England

General: Due to modern farming methods and draining of water meadows this delicate and beautiful plant has been eradicated from large areas of the countryside. However, it may still be found in quite large numbers in a few wet meadows in southern and central England. Fortunately, it is a fairly popular cultivated species and is often to be seen in private and public gardens. *Fritillaria* is from the Latin word *fritillus* (dice-box) and refers to the delicate chequered patterning on the petals

Drone Fly
Hover Fly
Eristalis (Plate 23)

This is another of the two-winged flies and is very similar to the honey-bee in colouration – the two can often be seen feeding together on the same flowers. It can be found on the wing from late spring until well into the autumn. Although it is a very good flier and a delight to watch in its controlled flight, it is another of the 'occasional' flies that from time to time are blown or fall on to the water surface. *E. tenax* produces the larval stage known as the rat-tailed maggot and a more apt and descriptive name would be difficult to think up. The maggot lives in the decaying matter to be found in still waters, the tail acting as a tube through which it can breathe. The maggot reaches a length of 20mm; the adult 13mm. Patterns exist for both stages.

Dressings

1. Drone Fly (Walker)

DRESSING

Hook length: 10mm
Thread: Brown
Abdomen: Yellow wool to shape
Rib: Black wool
Thorax: Black wool
Wing: Blue dun cock hackle tips tied over abdomen
Hackle: Yellow cock

2. Drone Fly (Inwood)

DRESSING

Hook length: 10mm
Thread: Red
Abdomen: Yellow chenille to shape
Rib: Bronze peacock herl
Wing: White cock hackle tips tied split and rear sloping over abdomen
Hackle: Medium brown cock
Head: Tying thread

3. Rat-Tailed Maggot (Walker)

DRESSING

Hook length: 12mm
Thread: Grey
Abdomen: Hare's ear mixed with fluorescent white wool
Breathing tube: Bleached cock pheasant tail fibre

4. Rat-Tailed Maggot (Price)

DRESSING

Hook length: 12mm
Thread: Grey
Abdomen: Grey fur and small amount of white fluorescent wool
Abdomen cover: Latex
Rib: Black thread
Breathing tube: Stripped hackle stalk

5. Rat-Tailed Maggot (Thomas)

DRESSING

Hook length: 12mm
Thread: Grey
Abdomen: White fluorescent wool
Rib: Stripped cock hackle stalk
Thorax: Brown ostrich herl
Breathing tube: White swan fibres

Common Duckweed
Duckmeat, Frog's Buttons
Lemna minor (Plate 23)
Duckweed family (*Lemnaceae*)

Flower head: Minute flowers, rarely produced, that have neither petals nor sepals, consisting of just two stamens and a small ovary

Leaves: Round, floating, leaflike fronds up to 8mm across, each having a single root
Flowering time: June–August
Habit: Perennial
Habitat: Ponds and ditches, stagnant and slow-flowing waters
Distribution: Common
General: This tiny, floating aquatic plant spreads so rapidly that it becomes a nuisance in many places; once established it is difficult to eradicate. The small, leaflike fronds or thalli continually divide to produce new ones, forming huge masses that totally cover the surface of the water. It is eaten readily by wild fowl, hence its common name 'duckmeat', and has been tried as fodder for animals

Plate 23

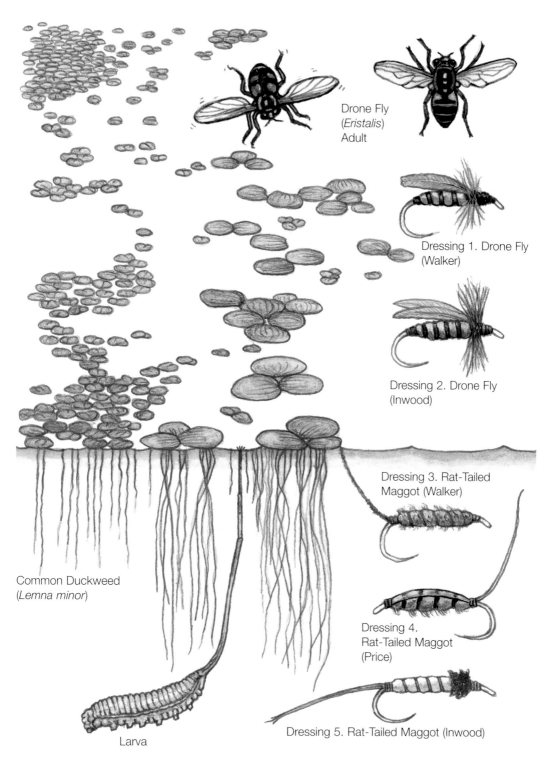

Drone Fly
(*Eristalis*)
Adult

Dressing 1. Drone Fly
(Walker)

Dressing 2. Drone Fly
(Inwood)

Dressing 3. Rat-Tailed
Maggot (Walker)

Common Duckweed
(*Lemna minor*)

Dressing 4.
Rat-Tailed Maggot
(Price)

Larva

Dressing 5. Rat-Tailed Maggot (Inwood)

Reed Smut
Black Fly
Simulium (Plate 24)

This is an extremely common species, usually dark brown or black in colour and very small and stockily built. Hatches occur throughout the summer months and the small larvae, which are found clinging to underwater objects, are present in such great numbers that trout can be seen sipping them down contentedly, often ignoring larger mouthfuls that may be hatching off at the same time. Because of the difficulty in tying an artificial to match them, they have also been named the 'black curse' but the important thing to remember when fishing them is to persevere and to try and place your fly in the expected path of a feeding trout. The larva grows to about 10mm in length, is grey-green in colour, has a club-shaped body and is found in running water. The pupa is about 8mm long with exaggerated breathing filaments that form a silken cocoon. The adult can grow up to 6mm in length but most are about 3mm.

Dressings

1. Smut (Goddard)

DRESSING

Hook length: 6mm
Thread: Black
Abdomen: Ostrich herl to front half of hook
Hackle: Very short-fibred black cock

2. Smut (Mottram)

DRESSING

Hook length: 6mm
Thread: Black
Abdomen: Black floss silk with a silver tip, all tied on front half of hook
Hackle: Starling breast feather

3. Smut (Price)

DRESSING

Hook length: 6mm
Thread: Grey
Abdomen: Oak turkey fibres
Hackle: Very small badger cock

4. Reed Smut

DRESSING

Hook length: 6mm
Thread: Black
Abdomen: Black feather fibres or tying thread
Wing: Smallest white feather tips
Throat hackle: Dark red game

5. Smut (Jacobsen)

DRESSING

Hook length: 6mm silver
Thread: Brown
Abdomen: Blood-red cow's hair over copper wire with a silver tip at both ends

Plate 24

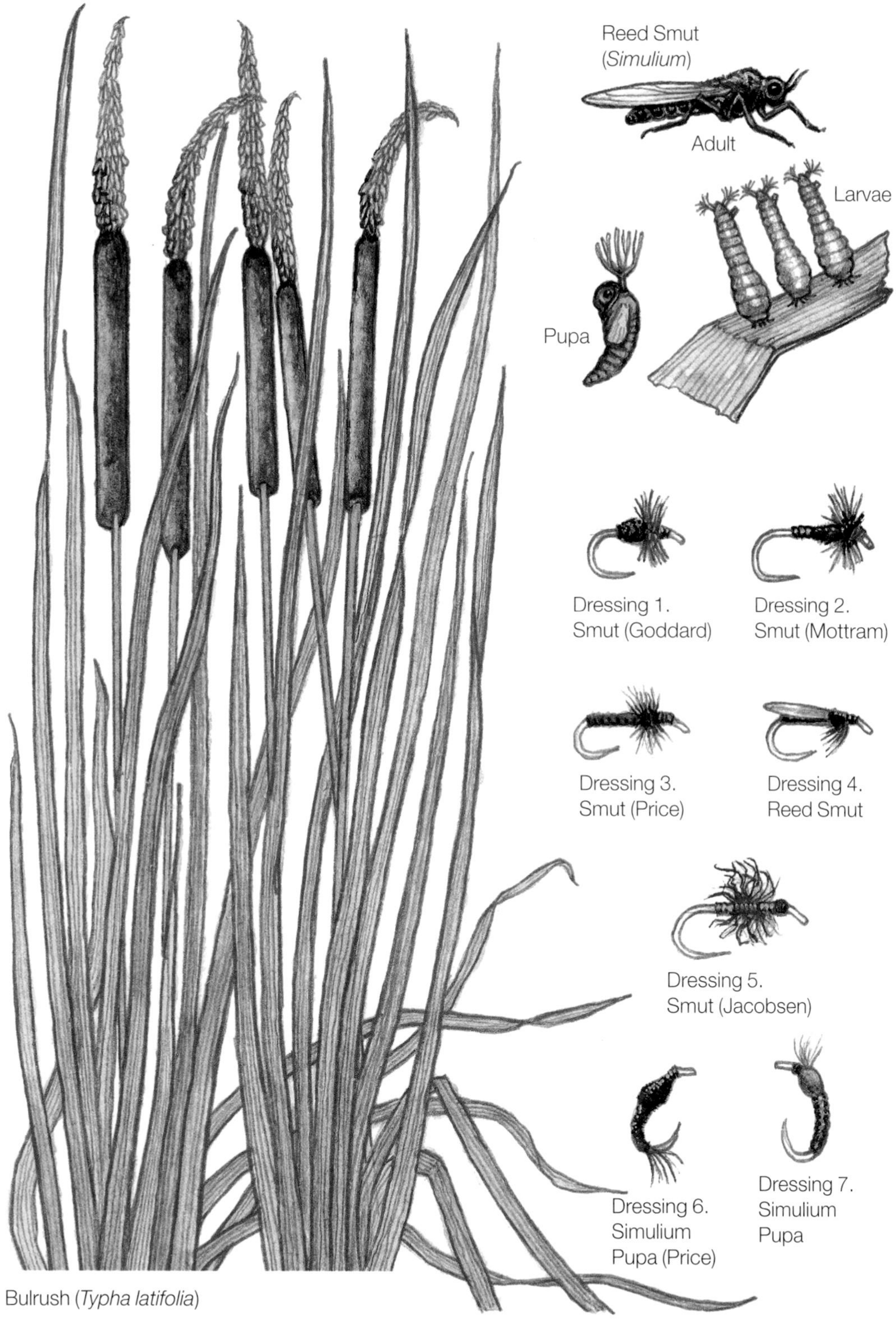

Reed Smut
(*Simulium*)
Adult

Larvae

Pupa

Dressing 1.
Smut (Goddard)

Dressing 2.
Smut (Mottram)

Dressing 3.
Smut (Price)

Dressing 4.
Reed Smut

Dressing 5.
Smut (Jacobsen)

Dressing 6.
Simulium
Pupa (Price)

Dressing 7.
Simulium
Pupa

Bulrush (*Typha latifolia*)

6. Simulium Pupa (Price)

DRESSING

Hook length: 6mm
Thread: Black
Tail: A few cock hackle fibres
Abdomen: Tying thread built to shape over
copper wire

7. Simulium Pupa

DRESSING

Hook length: 6mm curved
Thread: Black
Abdomen: Black thread
Thorax: Very fine tan dubbing
Breathing filaments: Fine white feather fibres

Bulrush
Nailrod, Cat's Tail, Common Reed Mace
Typha latifolia (Plate 24)
Reed mace family (*Typhaceae*)

Flower head:	A brown, sausage-shaped flower head of tiny female flowers, tightly packed together with a male flower head rising from the top to form a long, cylindrical flower spike
Leaves:	Erect, straight-edged sword-like leaves, greyish-green in colour, up to 20mm across and mostly basal

Flowering time:	June–July
Height:	Up to 2.5m
Habit:	Perennial
Habitat:	Wet, swampy ground, pond sides and edges of slow-moving rivers
Distribution:	Common throughout except Scotland
General:	The bulrush is one of twelve species of reed mace. It is a familiar sight at watersides where it forms huge colonies that are present throughout the year, even in the harshest of winters. Initially, male and female flower spikes appear together, but then the male flower head withers away leaving the familiar brown cigar-shaped female spike. Various parts of the plant may be eaten including the young shoots and flower heads. The leaves, which are waterproof, were once used in making reed boats and for weaving into baskets, chairs and mats. The seeds, which have a covering of fluffy hairs, were used to stuff mattresses

Beetles (Aquatic)
Coleoptera (Plate 25)

The illustration shows a range of aquatic beetles and larvae, which, unlike terrestrial beetles, spend all or part of their life in water for which many are especially adapted. In some, the legs have developed into oar-like appendages that allow them to move about efficiently through the water or skull about on the surface. Two prime examples of this are the voracious great diving beetle and the more diminutive whirligig beetle. In the former, the last pair of legs have developed to enable it to move through the water very quickly, in the latter the legs have practically been replaced by two tiny oars that speed it about on the water surface. Not all aquatic beetles have developed in this way though; the riffle beetle has normal legs and does not swim but merely crawls about on stones and aquatic vegetation. The larvae can vary quite considerably in shape and size but the colourations are very similar, usually shades of brown. Depending on species, they can be found in most fishing locations. However, most patterns have been designed with terrestrial beetles in mind.

Dressings
1. Dytiscus Larva (Price)

DRESSING

Hook length: 20mm swimming hook or longshank, bent
Thread: Brown
Tail: Brown hackle fibres
Abdomen: Dirty yellow dubbing wick
Rib: Abdomen area is ribbed with clear nylon
Thorax: As abdomen
Wing case and back: Thorax and abdomen covered with strip of brown PVC
Legs: Brown partridge tied in flat under wing case
Head: Synthetic brown dubbing to form ball shape
Eyes: Black beads

2. Black and Peacock Spider (Ivens)

DRESSING

Hook length: Up to 14mm
Thread: Black
Abdomen: Bronze peacock herl
Hackle: Black hen

3. Beetle Larva

DRESSING

Hook length: Up to 12mm
Thread: Brown
Tail: Short brown fibres
Abdomen: Fine pale brown dubbing tied slim
Legs: Very short pale brown hackle palmered full length and cut short to body shape

4. Black Beetle (Fogg)

DRESSING

Hook length: Up to 10mm
Thread: Brown
Abdomen: Black ostrich herl
Tip: Silver tinsel
Wing case: Black raffene pulled over abdomen
Hackle: Black cock

5. Chomper (Walker)

DRESSING

Hook length: Up to 12mm
Thread: Black
Abdomen: Peacock herl
Wing case: Black raffene over abdomen

6. Red-Eyed Derbyshire Beetle (Hardy)

DRESSING

Hook length: Up to 12mm
Thread: Black
Abdomen: Bronze peacock herl
Hackle: Black hen
Eyes: Red beads

7. Beetle

DRESSING

Hook length: Up to 12mm
Thread: Dark grey
Abdomen: Charcoal-grey seal's fur sub to shape
Thorax: As abdomen
Thorax and wing case cover: Black raffene pulled over and tied to shape
Legs: Black hackle fibres

Water Soldier
Stratiotes aloides (Plate 25)
Frogbit family (*Hydrocharitaceae*)

Flower head:	White flowers up to 4cm wide. Male and female flowers are on separate plants. Female flowers are solitary and on a short stalk, whereas several male flowers may be found on one stem
Leaves:	Narrow leaves up to 45cm long with spiny-toothed margins, form a basal rosette. Leaves are triangular in cross-section
Flowering time:	June–August
Height:	Up to 45cm
Habit:	Perennial
Habitat:	Ponds, ditches and lakes
Distribution:	Locally common in eastern England, rarer elsewhere
General:	The water soldier is an aquatic perennial mostly found in waters rich in nutrients yet low in chalk, the male plant of the species being much more rare than the female. It stays mostly submerged at the bottom, only floating to the top at flowering time

Plate 25

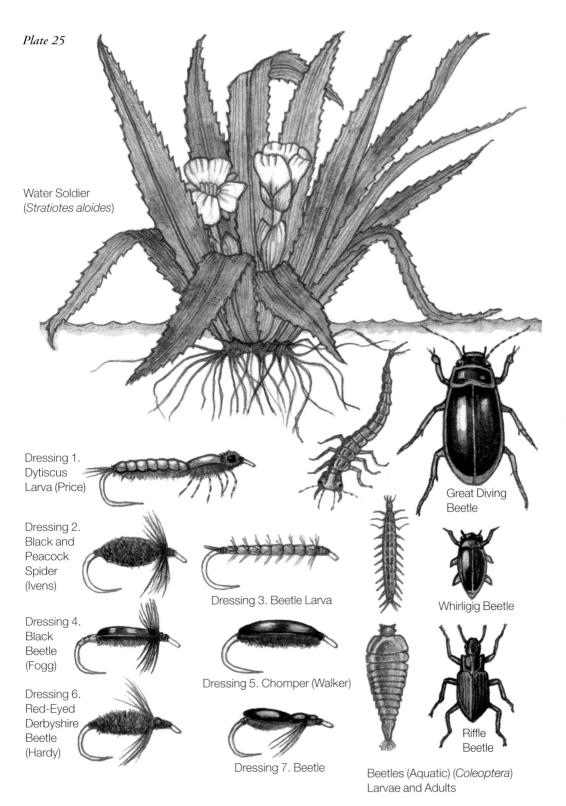

Water Soldier
(*Stratiotes aloides*)

Dressing 1.
Dytiscus
Larva (Price)

Dressing 2.
Black and
Peacock
Spider
(Ivens)

Dressing 3. Beetle Larva

Dressing 4.
Black
Beetle
(Fogg)

Dressing 5. Chomper (Walker)

Dressing 6.
Red-Eyed
Derbyshire
Beetle
(Hardy)

Dressing 7. Beetle

Great Diving
Beetle

Whirligig Beetle

Riffle
Beetle

Beetles (Aquatic) (*Coleoptera*)
Larvae and Adults

Daphnia
(Plate 26)

It is said that on some of the larger reservoirs this very tiny and abundant crustacean can be one of the main sources of food available to trout. However, as the largest are only about 3mm long, the tying and fishing of an artificial is impossible. But because trout can become preoccupied with swimming and feeding in these clouds of daphnia, which move up and down at various depths in the water taking the fish with them, the stillwater angler can use them as an indicator as to the depth at which the fish are feeding. The skilled reservoir angler has learnt that at this time an orange or lime-green coloured lure, nymph or wet fly will pay dividends. The daphniidae range in colour from red to green and all the shades in between and this must account for the brighter coloured 'fly' working under these conditions.

Dressings

1. Orange Nymph (Price)

DRESSING

Hook length: 10mm
Thread: Orange
Abdomen: Orange synthetic fur
Abdomen back: Goose-dyed orange with two tufts left at eye end
Rib: Oval gold tinsel, back is then varnished

2. Orange Nymph (Cove)

DRESSING

Hook length: 12mm
Thread: Orange
Abdomen: Orange seal's fur sub
Rib: Gold tinsel
Thorax: As abdomen
Wing case: Pheasant tail fibres

3. Partridge and Orange

DRESSING

Hook length: 12mm
Thread: Orange
Rib: Gold wire
Hackle: Brown partridge

4. Green DF Partridge (Walker)

DRESSING

Hook length: 12mm
Thread: Black
Abdomen: Lime-green DF wool to shape
Rib: Silver wire
Hackle: Brown partridge

5. Lime Pheasant Tail (Church)

DRESSING

Hook length: Up to 20mm
Thread: Brown
Tail: Cock pheasant fibres
Abdomen: Cock pheasant fibres
Rib: Gold wire
Thorax: Fluorescent lime-green
Wing case: Cock pheasant fibres
Legs: Tips of wing case

Plate 26

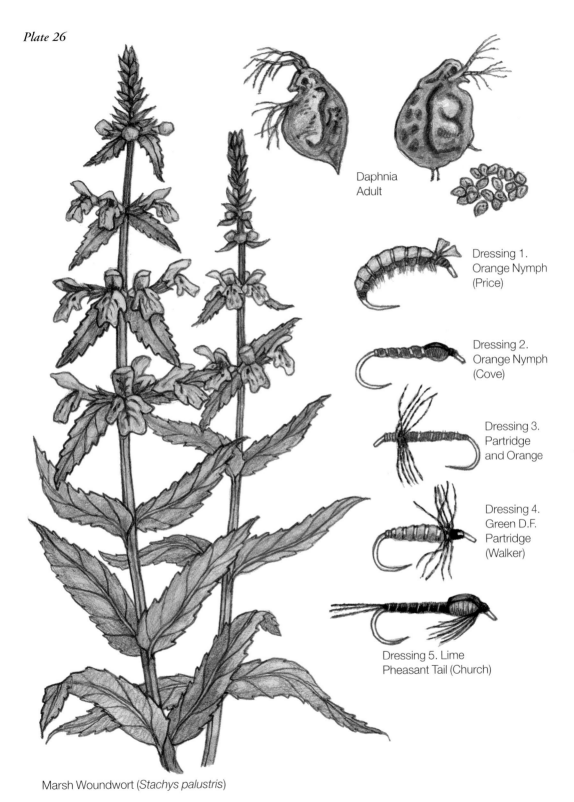

Daphnia
Adult

Dressing 1.
Orange Nymph
(Price)

Dressing 2.
Orange Nymph
(Cove)

Dressing 3.
Partridge
and Orange

Dressing 4.
Green D.F.
Partridge
(Walker)

Dressing 5. Lime
Pheasant Tail (Church)

Marsh Woundwort (*Stachys palustris*)

Marsh Woundwort
Marsh Betony
Stachys palustris (Plate 26)
Mint family (*Labiatae*)

Flower head:	Dull purple or mauve flowers carried in whorls of six in a loose spike at the top of the stem
Leaves:	Lance-shaped, stalkless leaves with serrated edges, 5–12cm long, rise from the stem in opposite pairs
Flowering time:	July–September
Height:	Up to 1m
Habit:	Perennial
Habitat:	Ditches, swamps, fens, streams and ponds
Distribution:	Common except in parts of the north

General: Marsh woundwort has been valued for centuries for its antiseptic properties. It was also used to heal wounds and stem the flow of blood. John Gerrard, a sixteenth-century herbalist, was most impressed when a labourer demonstrated these healing qualities to him. He observed that by applying a clean poultice of fresh leaves every day the labourer's wound healed much faster than would be expected using traditional healing methods. Young shoots, which are similar to asparagus, may be picked and eaten as a vegetable

Shrimp
Gammarus (Plate 27)

Shrimp, another staple food source of trout, are always present in water systems whether moving or static. When other, tastier life forms are available, the trout will have a preference for these, but when they are less in evidence then shrimp come into their own and although not a true 'fly' as such should have a place in every fly-fisherman's box. It is preferable to have two colours, olive-grey and sandy-orange. Olive-grey is the normal colour of the shrimp but at mating time during the warmer summer months the colour changes to sandy-orange. The males are larger than the females and during mating will ride in tandem for several days on the female's back. All shrimp are curved in appearance and have many limbs that are capable of different functions. Movement is in short, sharp jerks, usually with the shrimp swimming on its side. Fully grown shrimp range in size from 12–18mm.

Dressings

1. Shrimp (Walker)

DRESSING

Hook length: 15mm curved
Thread: Olive
Abdomen: Built up with lead to give shape then covered with wound olive wool
Legs: A palmered ginger over abdomen, only underside fibres remain, others trimmed away
Back: Coats of clear varnish

2. Shrimp (Hoskin)

DRESSING

Hook length: 15mm curved
Thread: Maroon
Abdomen: Built up with lead, seal's fur sub, olive and orange (3:1) picked out for legs
Rib: Oval gold tinsel
Back: Two layers of polythene, bottom layer ribbed with tinsel then other layer pulled over
Feelers: A few olive cock hackle fibres tied in at eye pointing up and forwards

3. Shrimp (Edwards)

DRESSING

Hook length: 15mm curved
Thread: Grey
Abdomen: Built up with lead, covered with olive fur and grey partridge fibres dubbed together
Rib: Nylon mono about 4lb BS
Back: Clear polythene
Feelers and legs: Grey partridge fibres

4. Red Spot Shrimp (Patterson)

DRESSING

Hook length: 15mm curved
Thread: Olive
Abdomen: Built up with lead, covered with olive seal's fur sub and olive mohair, spot of red fluorescent wool incorporated in a central position
Rib: Gold wire
Legs: Picked out body fur
Back: Double layer of clear polythene

5. Mating Shrimp (Goddard)

DRESSING

Hook length: 15mm curved
Thread: Orange
Abdomen: Built up with lead covered with seal's fur sub, olive, dark brown and fluorescent pink (6:3:1)
Rib: Silver wire
Legs: Picked out body fur
Back: Clear polythene

6. Grayling Bug (Sawyer)

DRESSING

Hook length: 15mm curved
Thread: Copper wire
Abdomen: Built up copper wire covered with beige wool
Rib: Copper wire to give segmented shape

Fool's Watercress
Marshwort
Apium nodiflorum (Plate 27)
Umbellifer family (*Umbelliferae*)

Flower head:	Groups of flowers with either no stalk or very short stalks form umbrella-shaped flower heads that join the stem opposite a leaf
Leaves:	Stalkless, shiny, bright green leaflets with serrated edges are in opposite pairs on the stem with a terminal leaflet at the end
Flowering time:	July–August
Height:	Up to 90cm
Habit:	Perennial
Habitat:	Marshy places; shallow, still or slow-moving rivers and streams
Distribution:	Throughout
General:	Fool's watercress loves muddy situations but also thrives in nutrient-rich streams on chalky or limestone soils. It is very similar in appearance to true watercress, hence its name, and like watercress it can be eaten. In some areas it was cooked with meat and added to pies. The herbalist, Culpepper, recommended it as a drink for those on a diet

Plate 27

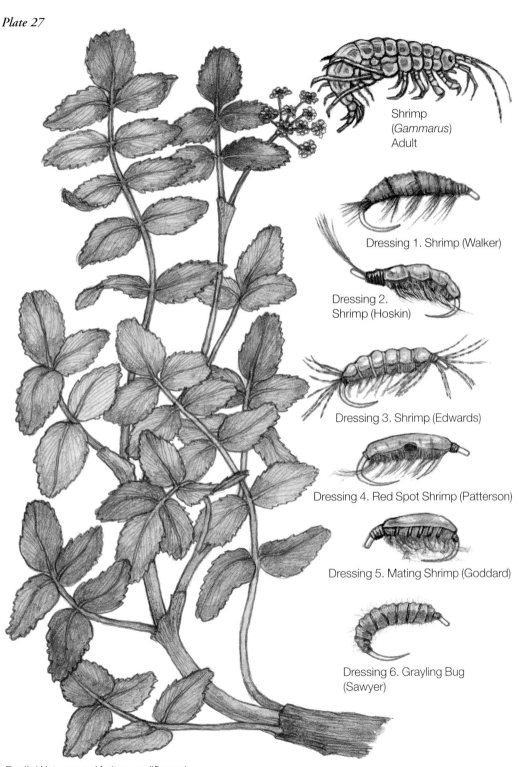

Shrimp
(*Gammarus*)
Adult

Dressing 1. Shrimp (Walker)

Dressing 2.
Shrimp (Hoskin)

Dressing 3. Shrimp (Edwards)

Dressing 4. Red Spot Shrimp (Patterson)

Dressing 5. Mating Shrimp (Goddard)

Dressing 6. Grayling Bug
(Sawyer)

Fool's Watercress (*Apium nodiflorum*)

Snails (Gastropods)
(Plate 28)

Snails can be found in most water systems and vary little in shape or colour. The shell shows some form of a spiral shape and the overall colour is a shade of brown with touches of yellow and green. Most of their time is spent wandering over the bottom or amongst weeds where they can be picked off by scavenging trout. Occasionally, during periods of hot weather, there will be a migration of large numbers of snails to the water surface where they hang upside-down with their 'foot' in the surface film. It is at these times that trout will take them in large numbers. Most of the artificial 'flies' designed for snails are quite basic and very simple to tie.

Dressings

1. Spiral Snail

DRESSING

Hook length: 16mm
Thread: Silver wire
Abdomen: Brown cork cut to shape with a spiral groove and glued to hook
Rib: Silver tip left at rear then silver brought to run up spiral cut in cork
Head: A few turns of peacock herl

2. Snail (Church)

DRESSING

Hook length: 16mm
Thread: Black or brown chenille
Abdomen: Tying thread built into shape

3. Snail (Henry)

DRESSING

Hook length: 16mm
Thread: Black
Abdomen: Shaped cork covered in stripped peacock-eye quill
Head: Two turns of bronze peacock

4. Black and Peacock Spider (Ivens)

DRESSING

Hook length: 16mm
Thread: Black
Abdomen: Bronze peacock herl to shape
Hackle: Black hen

5. Upside-Down Snail (Barker)

DRESSING

Hook length: Up to 16mm with wide gape
Thread: Black
Abdomen: Dome-shaped coloured cork to shape, slit to take hook shank and glued in place. A small hole is made to take a round shot, this is glued in place and the extra weight makes the snail float upside-down in the manner of the natural

Plate 28

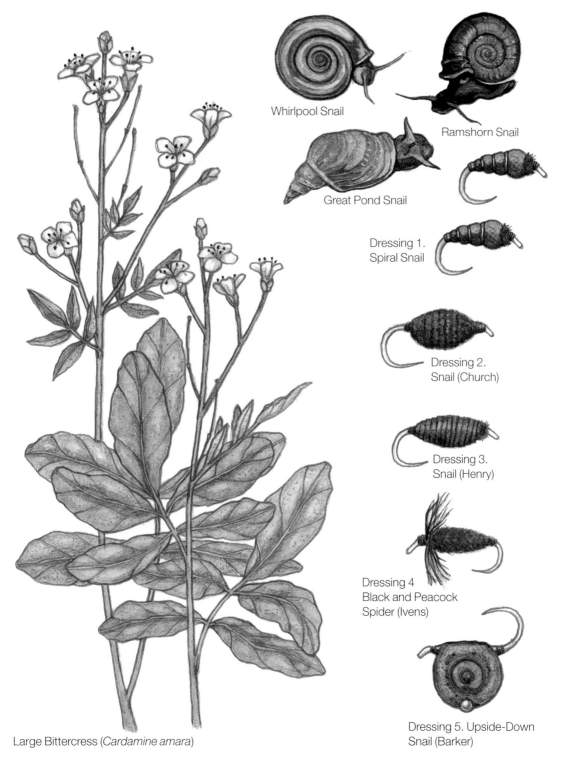

Snails (Gastropods)

Whirlpool Snail

Ramshorn Snail

Great Pond Snail

Dressing 1.
Spiral Snail

Dressing 2.
Snail (Church)

Dressing 3.
Snail (Henry)

Dressing 4
Black and Peacock
Spider (Ivens)

Dressing 5. Upside-Down
Snail (Barker)

Large Bittercress (*Cardamine amara*)

Large Bittercress
Cardamine amara (Plate 28)
Mustard family (*Cruciferae*)

Flower head:	Usually white but occasionally purple and carried in loose clusters. Flowers are 12mm across and made up of four petals in a cross shape
Leaves:	Alternate leaves, carried in pairs of between two and five oval leaflets, narrowing towards the top of the stem
Flowering time:	April–June

Height:	Up to 60cm
Habit:	Perennial
Habitat:	Wet meadows, river and stream margins
Distribution:	Common
General:	Large bittercress is a plant that thrives best in wet, nutrient-rich soils. It is typical of the mustard family to which it belongs, in having four petals in a cross shape. In appearance it is similar to, and is often confused with, watercress. It has a sharp, acrid taste but can be eaten, usually raw in salads

Greater Water Boatman
Notonecta

Lesser Water Boatman
Corixa (Plate 29)

Both species share the same common name despite having different habits. The greater water boatman is a true backswimmer having back legs so designed as to push it powerfully through the water in a jerking motion. It is often seen hanging at the water surface in an angled, upside-down position. In this way it can pick up any vibrations made by unsuspecting prey, such as insects or even small fish, which it will then attack with ferocity. The greater water boatman is a reasonably strong flier and in the summer months will often take to the air to seek out new territories in still or slow-moving areas of water. Coloured in shades of brown and green with creamy coloured undersides, it can attain a length of 16mm.

The lesser water boatman is basically the same shape but does not travel upside-down and spends very little time at the water surface. It is generally found at the bottom, feeding on algae that it scrapes off by means of specially adapted forelegs. When travelling between the bottom and the surface of the water it can move at incredible speed propelled along by its oar-like rear legs. In the summer it too will take flight to seek out and populate new territories. Coloured in shades of brown and green with creamy coloured undersides, it can grow to about 13mm.

Dressings

1. Silver Corixa (Price)

DRESSING

Hook length: 13mm
Thread: Brown
Abdomen: Flat silver lurex
Rib: Oval silver tinsel
Wing case: Cock pheasant tail fibres varnished
Paddles/rear legs: Two cock pheasant fibres tied in either side

2. Large Brown Corixa (Walker)

DRESSING

Hook length: 16mm
Thread: Black
Abdomen: White floss silk
Rib: Silver tinsel
Wing case: Brown speckled turkey
Paddles: Two turkey fibres tied in either side

3. Corixa (Dawes)

DRESSING

Hook length: 13mm
Thread: Brown
Abdomen: White floss
Rib: Tying thread
Wing case: Cock pheasant fibres
Paddles: Two cock pheasant fibres

4. Plastazote Corixa (Collyer)

DRESSING

Hook length: 13mm
Thread: Brown
Abdomen: Shaped piece of plastozote glued on to shank of hook
Wing case: Pheasant tail fibres
Paddles: Pheasant tail fibres

5. Corixa (Fogg)

DRESSING

Hook length: 13mm
Thread: Brown
Abdomen: Pale lemon angora wool
Rib: Silver wire
Tag: Silver
Wing case: Raffia stretched over abdomen and coloured with brown waterproof marker to give shaded effect
Paddles: Two bunches of brown feather fibres tied in each side

6. Green Corixa (Cove)

DRESSING

Hook length: 13mm
Thread: Olive
Abdomen: White terylene
Rib: Silver wire
Wing case: Cock pheasant fibres dyed olive-green
Paddles: Green feather fibres

Bog Asphodel
Maidenhair
Narthecium ossifragum
(Plate 29)
Lily family (*Liliacae*)

Flower head:	Up to twenty star-shaped, scented, bright yellow flowers carried in a fairly compact spike. Each flower has six petals and orange woolly stamens
Leaves:	Long and slender grass-like leaves, sometimes curved, grow from the base. Shorter leaves form sheaths around the stem
Flowering time:	July–September
Height:	10–40cm
Habit:	Perennial
Habitat:	Wet, peaty soils
Distribution:	Widespread and common in suitable conditions in the north and west, localized in the south and absent from East Anglia and the Midlands
General:	A hairless, creeping perennial that is often seen in July as a mass of fragrant, yellow flowers on bogs and heaths. It is a very attractive plant, frequently used as a bog garden ornamental. After flowering, the petals, sepals and stem all turn a deep orange colour. In the past it was used as a substitute for saffron and also as a hair dye for women, hence its common name 'maidenhair'. The belief that it was poisonous to sheep and caused brittle bone disease in cattle has been proven to be incorrect

Plate 29

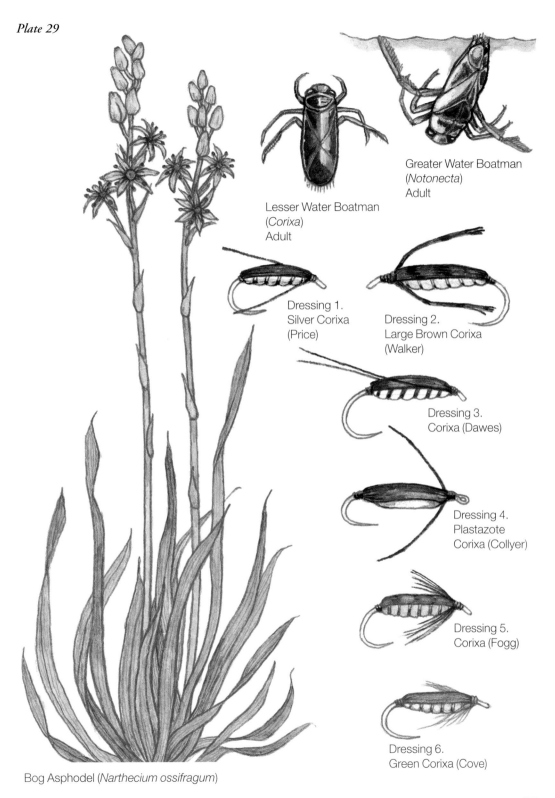

Greater Water Boatman
(*Notonecta*)
Adult

Lesser Water Boatman
(*Corixa*)
Adult

Dressing 1.
Silver Corixa
(Price)

Dressing 2.
Large Brown Corixa
(Walker)

Dressing 3.
Corixa (Dawes)

Dressing 4.
Plastazote
Corixa (Collyer)

Dressing 5.
Corixa (Fogg)

Dressing 6.
Green Corixa (Cove)

Bog Asphodel (*Narthecium ossifragum*)

Water Louse
Asellus Aquaticus,
A. meridianus (Plate 30)

In its features this is very similar to the woodlouse that is so common in the damp places around the garden. It spends much of its time roaming around on the river or lake bed searching out decaying animal and plant remains. Although it can be found in most types of still water and some rivers, it cannot, because of its design, tolerate fast flows. Where found, it can be very abundant and because of its slow movement is easily picked up by hungry fish. It has not received as much attention as the similar freshwater shrimp and consequently there are not as many patterns available. Because it moves slowly on the bottom, the artificial should be weighted and fished with a slow retrieve. The adult grows to about 15mm long and is a mottled grey-brown colour with a paler underbody.

Dressings

1. Water Louse (Bucknall)

DRESSING

Hook length: 13mm
Thread: Olive
Abdomen: Grey-olive fur or wool picked out at sides
Rib: Oval silver tinsel
Legs: Grey partridge fibres tied in two bunches at rear of abdomen

2. Water Louse (Gathercole)

DRESSING

Hook length: 13mm
Thread: Brown
Abdomen: Grey rabbit's fur
Rib: Silver wire
Legs: Brown partridge laid over abdomen, front fibres tied in bunches pointing forward, rear ones bunched to point backward
Back: Grey-brown feather fibres

3. Water Louse (Lapsley)

DRESSING

Hook length: 13mm
Thread: Brown
Abdomen: Mix of brown and grey hare fur trimmed on top and bottom
Rib: Silver tinsel
Legs: Abdomen picked out either side

4. Sow Bug (Whitlock)

DRESSING

Hook length: 13mm
Thread: Grey
Abdomen: Grey-brown fur and fibre
Rib: Gold wire
Legs: Abdomen fibres picked out
Back: Clear polythene strip
Feelers: Two grey duck biots

Plate 30

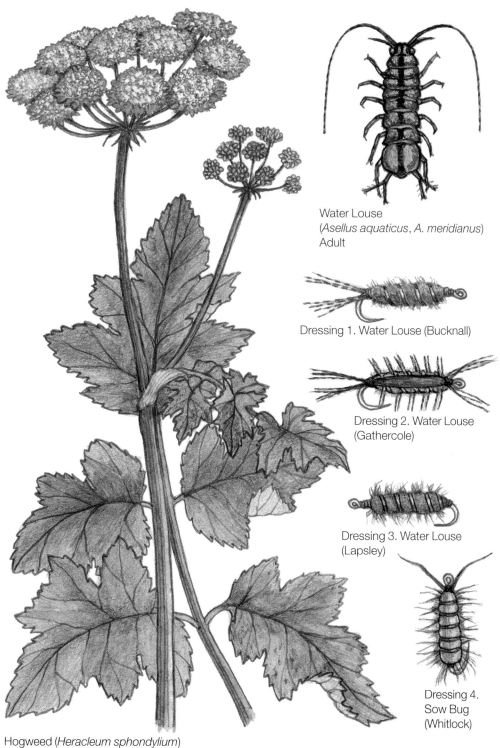

Water Louse
(*Asellus aquaticus*, *A. meridianus*)
Adult

Dressing 1. Water Louse (Bucknall)

Dressing 2. Water Louse
(Gathercole)

Dressing 3. Water Louse
(Lapsley)

Dressing 4.
Sow Bug
(Whitlock)

Hogweed (*Heracleum sphondylium*)

Hogweed
Cow Parsnip
Heracleum sphondylium
(Plate 30)
Umbellifer family (*Umbellifere*)

Flower head: Umbrella-shaped flower heads up to 15cm wide of white, sometimes pink, flowers 5–10mm across. The outer flowers have large, notched petals, the inner flowers are smaller

Leaves: Large basal leaves are lobed with toothed leaflets, the smaller upper leaves have inflated sheath-like bases. All leaves are hairy

Flowering time: June–September

Height: Up to 1.8m

Habit: Native perennial

Habitat: Woods, hedgerows, grassland, riverside meadows

Distribution: Common throughout

General: Named *Heracleum* after Hercules, the Greek hero, who had a strong belief in its medicinal properties, this erect, hairy plant is the most common species of the parsley family. The flowers, which give off an unpleasant smell, are often inhabited by bright orange soldier beetles, which like to make their home on them. Until recent times, the plant was gathered and fed to pigs, hence the common name 'hogweed'. The young leaves, when boiled, were considered to be a delicacy – somewhat like asparagus. The plant also contains a substance that can cause blisters if it comes into contact with the skin

Cranefly
Daddy-Longlegs
Tipula (Plate 31)

The cranefly is mainly to be found in late summer and autumn. They all have two wings with a very long body and legs – the more common species have grey-brown abdomens and clear wings, sometimes with brown blotches. If a cranefly is unfortunate enough to be blown on to the water, especially in lakes and reservoirs, a watchful trout will readily take it and because of this many patterns exist to imitate the winged insect. The larval stage of the cranefly is normally found in soil and is known, especially to gardeners, as a leatherjacket. Some species can be found in decaying vegetation or in debris at the bottom of moving and still waters, these tend to be the smaller species that are up to about 20mm long.

Dressings

1. Dyffryn Daddy (Hoskin)

DRESSING

Hook length: 12mm
Thread: Black or brown
Abdomen: Detached deer hair ribbed with tying thread
Thorax: Shaped ethafoam coloured brown
Wings: Cree hackle tips tied in semi-spent position
Legs: Knotted pheasant tail fibres

2. Cranefly (Walker)

DRESSING

Hook length: 17mm
Thread: Brown
Abdomen: Pale brown turkey fibres
Wings: Badger cock hackle points in 'V' shape over abdomen
Hackle: Pale ginger cock
Legs: Knotted cock pheasant fibres

3. Cranefly Larva (Price)

DRESSING

Hook length: 20mm
Thread: Black
Abdomen: Latex coloured grey with lead wire underneath
Rib: Gold wire
Hackle: Grey cock clipped short

Bird's Foot Trefoil
Lady's Shoes and Stockings, Crow Toes, Bacon and Eggs, Fingers and Thumbs
Lotus corniculatus (Plate 31)
Pea family (*Leguminosae*)

Flowering time:	June–September
Height:	Up to 50cm
Habit:	Perennial
Habitat:	Roadsides, grassy places, pastures
Distribution:	Common throughout
General:	Bird's foot trefoil is typical of the pea family of which it is a member. Although it is called trefoil meaning 'three-leafed', there are in fact five pairs of leaflets as one pair is carried very close to the stem. A variation of this plant is grown on the continent and used as a food source for animals

Flower head:	Loose clusters of between two and eight bright yellow flowers on stalks growing from leaf joints. The flowers, which are 1–1.5cm long, are often streaked red and slightly scented
Leaves:	Compound leaves made up of five pointed, sometimes fleshy, leaflets

Plate 31

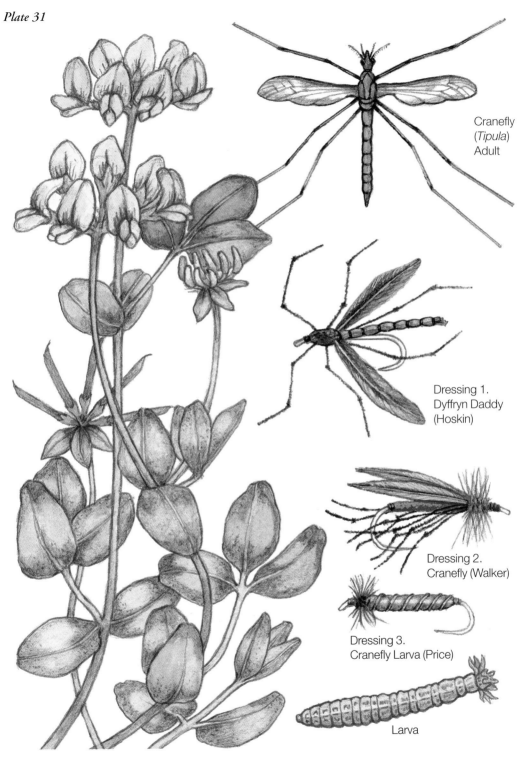

Cranefly
(*Tipula*)
Adult

Dressing 1.
Dyffryn Daddy
(Hoskin)

Dressing 2.
Cranefly (Walker)

Dressing 3.
Cranefly Larva (Price)

Larva

Bird's Foot Trefoil (*Lotus corniculatus*)

Moths and Caterpillars
Lepidoptera (Plate 32)

Most moths and their caterpillars are terrestrial creatures but some species, such as the china mark moth, have a partly aquatic life cycle. Fish seldom trouble the 'aquatic' moths because of the inaccessible places where their eggs are laid and because of the leaf-style cases their larvae live in. On the other hand, when, at the time of pupation, the catapillars lower themselves on silken threads so they dangle just above the water or when they become dislodged in breezy conditions and get blown on to the water, they will certainly catch the attention of the waiting trout. If there are sufficient numbers of caterpillars then the fish will gorge themselves, so a suitable imitation in green or brown is a must. Besides the larvae becoming available to trout, winged adults will also often get blown on to the surface and these too are readily taken. On warm, damp summer evenings, moths will be in evidence in fairly large numbers and several patterns have been tied to represent them.

Dressings

1. Coachman

DRESSING

Hook length: 12mm
Thread: Brown
Abdomen: Bronze peacock herl
Wing: White feather
Hackle: Red game cock

2. Ermine Moth

DRESSING

Hook length: 12mm
Thread: Black
Tail: Orange wool
Abdomen: Dubbed white wool
Rib: Tying thread or silver tinsel
Hackle: Grey partridge

3. Skittering Moth (Roberts)

DRESSING

Hook length: 12mm Swedish dry fly hook
Thread: White
Abdomen: Dubbed polypropylene pale grey fur
Wing: Deer hair, white or grey
Hackle: Cream cock

4. Green Caterpillar

DRESSING

Hook length: 15mm curved
Thread: Brown
Abdomen: Tag of tying thread at both ends then green floss to give segmented body
Legs: Palmered green cock at first, third and last segments, cut short

5. Chenille Grub (Fogg)

DRESSING

Hook length: 12mm
Thread: Black
Abdomen: Green or brown chenille tied in behind eye as a detached body

Plate 32

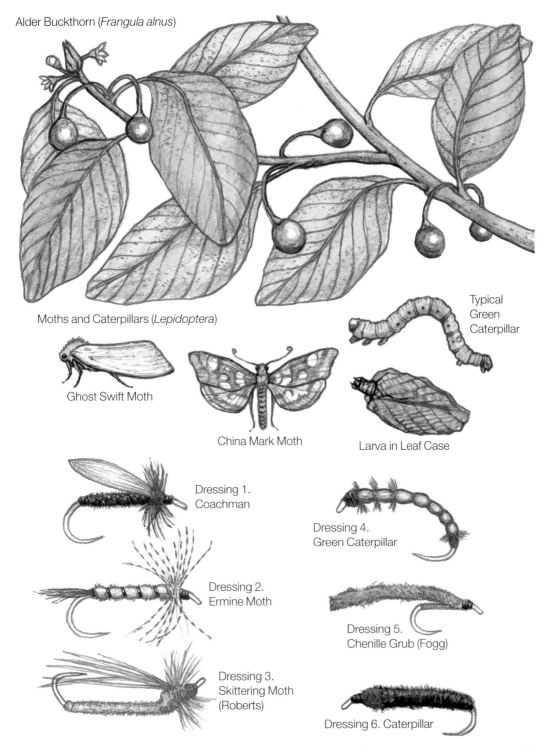

Alder Buckthorn (*Frangula alnus*)

Moths and Caterpillars (*Lepidoptera*)

Typical Green Caterpillar

Ghost Swift Moth

China Mark Moth

Larva in Leaf Case

Dressing 1. Coachman

Dressing 2. Ermine Moth

Dressing 3. Skittering Moth (Roberts)

Dressing 4. Green Caterpillar

Dressing 5. Chenille Grub (Fogg)

Dressing 6. Caterpillar

6. Caterpillar

Hook length: 15mm
Thread: Brown
Abdomen: Green or brown ostrich herl
Head: Peacock herl

Alder Buckthorn
Black Dogwood
Frangula alnus (Plate 32)
Buckthorn family (*Rhamnaceae*)

Flower head:	Several tiny greenish-coloured flowers appear at the junctions of leaf and twig
Leaves:	Leaves are alternate with between seven and nine pairs of parallel veins and smooth margins. They are a shiny green colour changing to yellow in autumn

Flowering time:	May–July
Height:	Up to 5m
Habit:	Native
Habitat:	Damp woods and bogs
Distribution:	Fairly common
General:	The name of this shrub is something of a misnomer, as it is neither related to the alder, although it frequently grows alongside it, nor does it have any thorns. It has had many and varied uses in the past. Until the end of the Second World War charcoal made from buckthorn was valued in the making of fuses due to its quality of burning slowly and evenly. Medicinally, the bark was used as a purgative and both bark and berries were used to induce vomiting. It is a hard wood that is easily sharpened and was favoured by butchers for making 'dogs' or skewers, hence its common name 'black dogwood'

Spiders (Aquatic and Terrestrial)
Arachnids (Plate 33)

Britain has only one truly aquatic spider and that is *Argyroneta aquatica*, the water spider, which is very similar to land-based spiders in most respects. Where it differs is in its ability to trap air in its body at the water surface and then transport it to underwater chambers specially constructed from silk threads that have been woven around several woody stems. The spider captures smaller insects by injecting them with poison and then carries them back to the relative safety of these air chambers where they can be devoured at leisure. The water spider can only be found in weedy ponds and areas of still water, but terrestrial spiders can be found around the margins of all types of water and at times they are easily dislodged or blown on to the water surface where they will readily be taken by a watchful trout. Most of these spiders occur in shades of brown and the patterns are designed to reflect this. Unfortunately, some confusion does arise with the northern style of artificial flies known as spider patterns that are not meant to represent any form of natural spider at all.

Dressings
1. Aquatic Spider

DRESSING

Hook length: 11mm
Thread: Black
Abdomen: Brown fur tied to shape
Tag: Silver tinsel
Legs: Dark brown cock hackle

2. Plastazote Spider

DRESSING

Hook length: 11mm
Thread: Dull yellow
Abdomen: Plastazote cut to shape and coloured brown
Tag: Silver tinsel
Legs: Cock pheasant fibres tied in behind thorax area

3. Windborne Spider (Price)

DRESSING

Hook length: 11mm
Thread: To match
Abdomen: Shaped body of red, brown or black polypropylene
Legs: Cock hackle tied in parachute style, coloured as for abdomen

4. Spider (Roberts)

DRESSING

Hook length: 11mm
Thread: Brown
Abdomen: Brown seal's fur sub
Tag and Rib: Silver tinsel
Legs: Brown partridge

Common Meadow Rue
Thalictrum flarum (Plate 33)
Buttercup family (*Ranunculaceae*)

Flower head:	The dense clusters of yellowish flowers at the end of tall stems have four tiny white petals and numerous yellow stamens
Leaves:	Deeply divided alternate leaves
Flowering time:	June–August
Height:	Up to 1m
Habit:	Perennial

Habitat:	Meadows, stream sides
Distribution:	Common
General:	This member of the familiar buttercup family has a liking for lime-rich soils. The flowers, which are totally unlike the rest of the family, give off a sweet-smelling perfume. Although the actual petals are white, they soon wither after the flower has opened and it is the many stamens that give the appearance of a yellow flower head

Plate 33

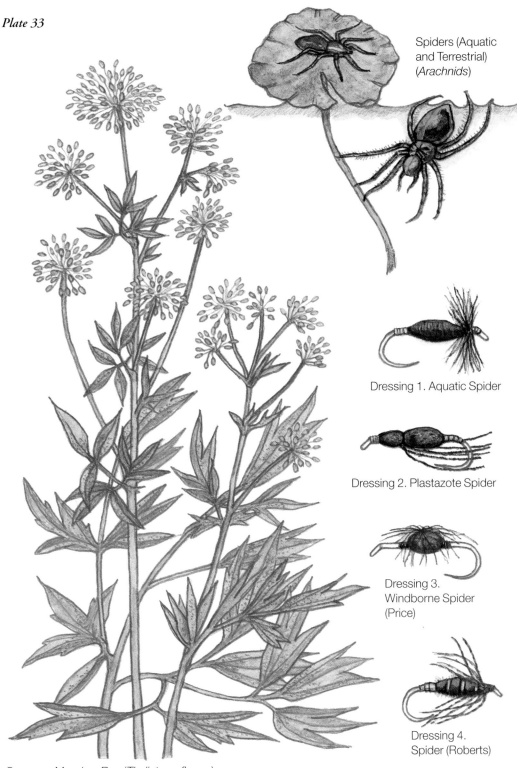

Spiders (Aquatic and Terrestrial) (*Arachnids*)

Dressing 1. Aquatic Spider

Dressing 2. Plastazote Spider

Dressing 3. Windborne Spider (Price)

Dressing 4. Spider (Roberts)

Common Meadow Rue (*Thalictrum flarum*)

PART 3

Miscellaneous 'Flies' (Terrestrial)

('Flies' that live all of their life cycles on land)

Ants
Formicidae (Plate 34)

Ants are rarely present on the water in sufficient numbers to cause any kind of a stir amongst trout. However, during mating time in the warmer summer months, they develop wings and become airborne and at this time they can be blown on to the water in sufficient numbers to trigger a large rise of trout. Of the many species of ant, the black garden ant, the wood ant and the meadow ant are some of the most common, they also represent the many variations in colour – black, red-brown and yellow.

Dressings

1. Plastazote Ant (Swanberg)

DRESSING

Hook length: 6mm
Thread: Black
Abdomen: Black plastazote to shape
Thorax: As abdomen
Legs: Black mono

2. Black Ant (Jardine)

DRESSING

Hook length: 6mm
Thread: Black
Abdomen: Black polypropylene
Thorax: As abdomen
Legs: Small black cock tied in between abdomen and thorax

3. Brown Ant (Goddard)

DRESSING

Hook length: 6mm
Thread: Brown
Abdomen: Shaped piece of cork
Thorax: As abdomen, then abdomen and thorax coloured and varnished
Wing: White cock hackle tips tied in central and slightly spent
Legs: Short brown cock hackle

4. Flying Ant (Jardine)

DRESSING

Hook length: 6mm
Thread: Brown
Abdomen: Brown seal's fur sub to shape
Thorax: As abdomen
Wing: Grey feather tips
Hackle: Short brown cock
Legs: A few small brown deer hair fibres tied in rear facing to represent trailing legs

Creeping Buttercup
Ranunculus repens (Plate 34)
Buttercup family (*Ranunculaceae*)

Flower head:	Five glossy yellow petals with erect sepals forming open flowers either held singly or in loose clusters
Leaves:	Hairy and long stalked, all divided into three lobes, the middle one of which projects beyond the other two on a short stalk
Flowering time:	May–September
Height:	Up to 50cm
Habit:	Perennial
Habitat:	Arable land, damp pastures

Distribution:	Common throughout
General:	This typical member of the buttercup family is very similar in appearance to the meadow buttercup except that it has a furrowed flower stalk. It is a mat-forming perennial that can often become a pest when present on cultivated land as it spreads quickly and easily. As it has an unpleasant taste and is slightly poisonous, it is not eaten by cattle and so it has the opportunity to spread rapidly where grass around it has been grazed. Once established it is difficult to eradicate

Plate 34

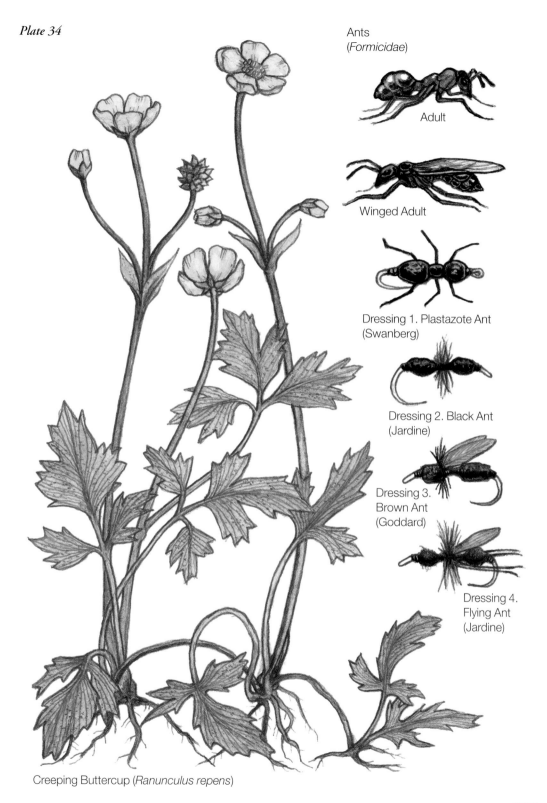

Ants
(*Formicidae*)

Adult

Winged Adult

Dressing 1. Plastazote Ant
(Swanberg)

Dressing 2. Black Ant
(Jardine)

Dressing 3.
Brown Ant
(Goddard)

Dressing 4.
Flying Ant
(Jardine)

Creeping Buttercup (*Ranunculus repens*)

Bees and Wasps
Hymenoptera
(Plate 35)

Although some authorities will tell you that trout do not take bees and wasps, this is simply not true. On more than one occasion I have observed trout take wasps that have somehow fallen on to the water surface. However, this must be an infrequent occurrence and they are not regarded as a particularly useful fly. They have no particular aversion to water, in fact towards the end of summer wasp nests often have to be avoided on the riverbank. As both bees and wasps are very strong fliers they are seldom windborne casualties and for this reason, although patterns do exist, they are usually precluded from the average fly-box. The basic pattern for both flies is similar with some variation in colour.

Dressings
1. Bee

DRESSING

Hook length: 12mm
Thread: Brown
Abdomen: Dark brown seal's fur sub or thread
Rib: Tan thread
Wing: Hen pheasant tied over abdomen
Hackle: Furnace cock

2. Deer Hair Bee

DRESSING

Hook length: 12mm
Thread: Black
Abdomen: Dark brown poly dubbing
Rib: Yellow thread
Wing: Deer hair

3. Wasp Fly

DRESSING

Hook length: 12mm
Thread: Yellow
Abdomen: Dark brown hair, mohair and black rabbit's fur mixed
Rib: Yellow thread
Wing: Grey mallard flat over abdomen
Hackle: Black cock

4. Wasp

DRESSING

Hook length: 12mm
Thread: Yellow
Abdomen: Black seal's fur sub to shape
Rib: Yellow thread
Thorax: As abdomen, no rib
Wing: Two grey hackle tips
Hackle: Ginger cock hackle

5. Wasp

DRESSING

Hook length: 12mm
Thread: Yellow
Abdomen: Magpie herl
Rib: Thin yellow wool
Wing: White hackle tips
Hackle: Black cock

Plate 35

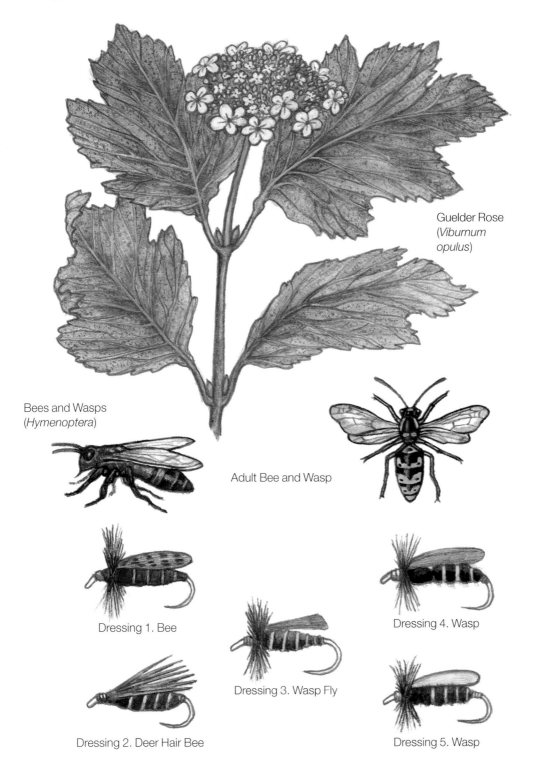

Guelder Rose
(*Viburnum opulus*)

Bees and Wasps
(*Hymenoptera*)

Adult Bee and Wasp

Dressing 1. Bee

Dressing 2. Deer Hair Bee

Dressing 3. Wasp Fly

Dressing 4. Wasp

Dressing 5. Wasp

119

Guelder Rose
Viburnum opulus (Plate 35)
Honeysuckle family (*Caprifoliaceae*)

Flower head: A dense, flatish head of small, white fertile flowers surrounded by larger infertile flowers

Leaves: Opposite leaves with between three and five lobes and deeply toothed margins. They are smooth on top but hairy beneath

Flowering time: May–June

Height: Up to 4m

Habit: Natural

Habitat: Damp, boggy areas and soil saturated by ground water

Distribution: Common in England and Wales, less so elsewhere

General: Four hundred years ago an unusual variety of the plant, which produced sterile flowers only, was found growing at Guelderland in Holland, hence the name. This attractive shrub was once referred to as 'swamp elder' or 'water elder' due to its preference for wet conditions and the resemblance to elderberries of the bunches of red berries produced in autumn. It can often be found growing alongside other moisture-loving plants such as sallow and alder. Cultivated varieties may often be seen in ornamental gardens but as bark, berries and leaves are all poisonous it is a plant to be treated with care

Beetles (Terrestrial)
Coleoptera (Plate 36)

There are so many different terrestrial beetles that it would need a specialist book to cover them all. However, I have tried to select the more common species and the ones that occur in sufficient numbers to make them useful from an angling point of view. Patterns are many and varied and although some are of a general nature, others are imitations of specific species. However, most patterns, even the ones tied to represent specific species, can usually be altered to represent most other forms.

Coch-y-bonddu Beetle
Cockchafer Beetle
(Plate 36)

These two beetles are very similar in colour and appearance but not in size so the only alteration to specific patterns would be size of hook. Both beetles are reasonably common and are on the wing in the early summer months; you are however much more likely to encounter the coch-y-bonddu as this is a day-flying species, the cockchafer prefers the evenings. Beetles are bulky creatures and when caught out by a sudden gust of wind can easily end up on the water surface. The wing case in both species is brown with a lighter underside; the thorax of the coch-y-bonddu is metallic green or black, whilst on the cockchafer it is shiny black. The coch-y-bonddu is approximately 12mm in length and the cockchafer about 25mm.

Dressings

1. Coch-y-bonddu (Old Welsh Dressing)

DRESSING

Hook length: 12mm
Thread: Black
Abdomen: Peacock herl
Tag: Gold tinsel
Hackle: Coch-y-bonddu cock hackle

2. Ethafoam Beetle (Warrilow)

DRESSING

Hook length: Up to 15mm
Thread: Brown
Abdomen: Brown seal's fur sub
Wing case: Ethafoam coloured brown and cut to shape
Hackle: Red game cock

3. Eric's Beetle (Horsfall Turner)

DRESSING

Hook length: Up to 12mm
Thread: Black
Abdomen: Bronze peacock to shape
Tag: Yellow wool
Hackle: Black cock or black hen

4. Brown Beetle

DRESSING

Hook length: 12mm
Thread: Brown
Abdomen: Brown seal's fur sub
Wing case: Brown feather fibres, varnished
Legs: Brown cock underside only

5. Beetle

DRESSING

Hook length: Up to 15mm
Thread: Brown
Abdomen: Dark brown or grey floss
Rib: On the grey floss abdomen rib with tying thread
Tag: Silver tinsel
Wing case: Raffene coloured brown and varnished
Hackle: Brown cock

Great Burnet
Burnet Bloodwort
Sanguisorba officinalio
(Plate 36)
Rose family (*Rosaceae*)

Flower head:	Dense, oblong-shaped heads are made up of numerous dark crimson flowers; there are no petals – the colouring comes from the sepals
Leaves:	Between three and seven pairs of toothed, long-stalked leaflets
Flowering time:	June–September
Height:	Up to 90cm
Habit:	Perennial
Habitat:	Damp pastures
Distribution:	Common in England and Wales
General:	This old herbal plant is one of a genus of eighteen perennial herbs and small shrubs. *Sanguisorba* (blood absorbing) refers to the use of parts of the plant for stemming the flow of blood from open wounds. When peeled, the root eases the pain from burns and encourages healing

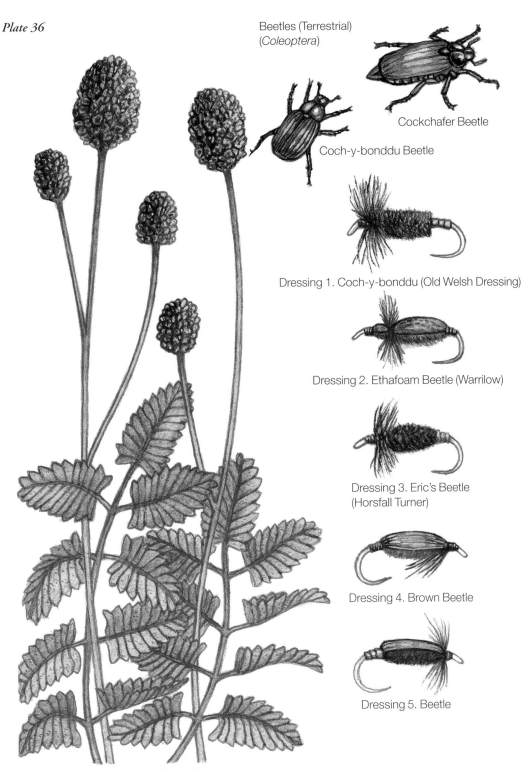

Plate 36

Beetles (Terrestrial)
(*Coleoptera*)

Cockchafer Beetle

Coch-y-bonddu Beetle

Dressing 1. Coch-y-bonddu (Old Welsh Dressing)

Dressing 2. Ethafoam Beetle (Warrilow)

Dressing 3. Eric's Beetle
(Horsfall Turner)

Dressing 4. Brown Beetle

Dressing 5. Beetle

Great Burnet (*Sanguisorba officinalio*)

Sailor Beetle
Cantharis rustica (Plate 37)

The sailor beetle, which got its name because of the resemblance of its colours to military uniforms of the nineteenth century, has dark blue-black wing cases and a red-orange thorax. In the summer months it may be found clambering around flower heads near still waters as well as rivers, preferring open meadow situations to underneath trees. Although a fairly common species, it is never present in the same numbers as the soldier beetle and it is not regarded as a particularly useful fly. This is reflected in the number of patterns that are available but they are so similar in shape and size that any of the soldier beetle patterns can be easily adapted by changing the colours of the materials used.

Dressings

1. Sailor Beetle (Price)

DRESSING

Hook length: 10mm
Thread: Black
Abdomen: Orange-brown floss
Wing case: Raffene coloured dark blue
Hackle: Black

2. Sailor Beetle

DRESSING

Hook length: 10mm
Thread: Orange
Abdomen: Bronze peacock herl
Tag: Orange thread
Hackle: Pale coch-y-bonddu or furnace

3. Sailor Beetle

DRESSING

Hook length: 10mm
Thread: Orange
Abdomen: Orange-brown seal's fur sub
Wing case: Blue-black feather fibres varnished
Hackle: Red game cock

4. Sailor Beetle

DRESSING

Hook length: 10mm
Thread: Black
Abdomen: Orange-brown dubbing
Thorax: Small round ball of dubbing
Wing case: Blue-black polythene over abdomen
Hackle: Red game cock

5. Beetle (based on Price's Black Beetle)

DRESSING

Hook length: 10mm
Thread: Black
Abdomen: Orange-brown polypropylene dub or seal's fur sub
Wing case: Blue-black raffene, varnished
Legs: Palmered black cock trimmed to leave downward sloping fibres

6. Foam Beetle

DRESSING

Hook length: 10mm
Thread: Black
Abdomen: Orange-brown seal's fur sub
Thorax: Orange ethafoam in ball shape
Wing case: Black ethafoam to shape over abdomen

Plate 37

Rowan (*Sorbus aucuparia*)

Sailor Beetle
(*Cantharis rustica*)

Dressing 1. Sailor Beetle (Price)

Dressing 4. Sailor Beetle

Dressing 2. Sailor Beetle

Dressing 5. Beetle (based on Price's Black Beetle)

Dressing 3. Sailor Beetle

Dressing 6. Foam Beetle

Rowan
Mountain Ash
Sorbus aucuparia (Plate 37)
Rose family (*Rosacaea*)

Flower head:	Dense clusters of small, strongly scented, creamy white flowers in a flower head 10–15cm across
Leaves:	Leaves first appear in April and consist of six or seven pairs of stalkless, toothed leaflets. The leaves, which are dark green above and paler below, rarely change colour before falling except in Scotland where they become bright crimson
Flowering time:	May
Height:	15–20m
Habit:	Native perennial
Habitat:	Rocky upland country but also common in parks and gardens

Distribution:	Common throughout
General:	A common, much-loved tree, easily identified by its dense clusters of white flowers in spring and its equally dense bunches of bright red berries in autumn. When the berries first appear they are yellow in colour but soon deepen through orange to the striking, bright red colour that makes them so attractive. When ripe they become a favourite food of blackbirds, thrushes and starlings, all of which may be seen devouring them greedily. The berries are also sometimes gathered and made into a somewhat smoky-flavoured jelly. When neither flowers nor fruit are present the tree may be identified by its attractive smooth bark, which is silvery-grey at first then turning to a light greyish-brown

Soldier Beetle
Cantharis livida (Plate 38)

In structure this beetle is exactly like the sailor beetle, but in appearance it has orange-brown wing cases with brownish-black tips to the rear and no black mark on the top of the thorax. It is a common species and can be found in large numbers on the flat type of flower heads such as cow parsley in the warm summer months. Like the sailor beetle it prefers open meadow situations and it is in these areas where it is most likely to be blown on to the water surface of rivers or lakes. If you doubt the usefulness of this type of fly, it must be remembered that it has stood the test of time – dressing 2 is testimony to this, it being from the fly-box of one G.E.M. Skues.

Dressings
1. Soldier Beetle (Price)

> **DRESSING**
>
> **Hook length:** 10mm
> **Thread:** Orange
> **Abdomen:** Mixed orange seal's fur sub, yellow seal's fur sub and small amount of hare's ear
> **Rib:** Black thread
> **Wing case:** Orange-brown raffene with black tip
> **Hackle:** Red cock

2. Soldier Beetle (Skues)

> **DRESSING**
>
> **Hook length:** 10mm
> **Thread:** Orange
> **Abdomen:** Red-orange seal's fur sub
> **Wing case:** Cock pheasant breast fibres
> **Hackle:** Red game cock hackle

3. Soldier Beetle

> **DRESSING**
>
> **Hook length:** 10mm
> **Thread:** Orange
> **Abdomen:** Orange seal's fur sub
> **Wing case:** Orange raffene with black tip varnished over
> **Legs:** Palmered red game cock

4. Foam Soldier Beetle

> **DRESSING**
>
> **Hook length:** 10mm
> **Thread:** Orange
> **Abdomen:** Orange polypropylene dubbing
> **Thorax:** Shaped fly foam coloured orange
> **Wing case:** Shaped fly foam coloured orange with black tip
> **Legs:** Ginger cock fibres tied in behind thorax

5. Soldier Beetle

> **DRESSING**
>
> **Hook length:** 10mm
> **Thread:** Orange
> **Abdomen:** Orange seal's fur sub
> **Rib:** Tying thread
> **Hackle:** Ginger cock

Sweet Flag
Sweet Rush
Acorus calanus (Plate 38)
Arum family (*Araceae*)

Flower head:	A densely packed spike of tiny, greenish-yellow flowers growing out at an angle of forty-five degrees from halfway up the flower stem
Leaves:	Very long, sword-like leaves up to 1m in length with wavy edges and pinkish at the base
Flowering time:	June–July
Height:	Up to 1m
Habit:	Introduced perennial
Habitat:	Margins of slow-moving rivers, canals, ponds and lakes
Distribution:	Localized throughout
General:	Sweet flag originated from India, which is still the only place where seedheads are produced, elsewhere it has to be propagated from the roots. It is an ancient plant that has been valued for centuries, in fact in Old Testament times an oil from the roots was used for anointing altars and sacred vessels. This same oil is still widely used in the manufacture of perfume and cosmetics. When crushed, the whole plant gives off a sweet smell of tangerines and cinnamon and was popular for strewing floors. It was also used as an insecticide and medicinally as a tonic and a cure for toothache

Plate 38

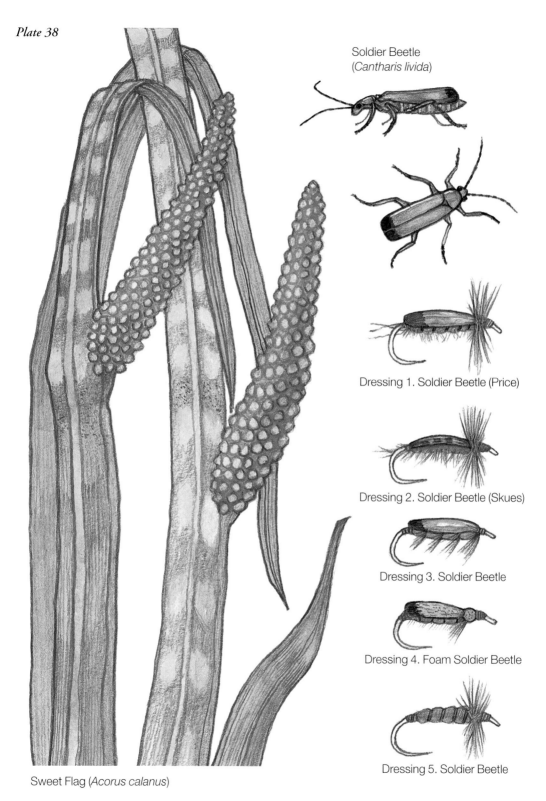

Soldier Beetle
(*Cantharis livida*)

Dressing 1. Soldier Beetle (Price)

Dressing 2. Soldier Beetle (Skues)

Dressing 3. Soldier Beetle

Dressing 4. Foam Soldier Beetle

Dressing 5. Soldier Beetle

Sweet Flag (*Acorus calanus*)

Black Gnat
Dilophus febrilis, Bibio johannis (Plate 39)

These are just two of the many flies known as black gnats. For angling purposes they have all been put under the same heading as the chief difference between species is mainly down to size. The patterns to represent these flies are many and varied but all have black as the basic colour. The naturals can be found throughout the fishing year but are usually more in evidence in the early and late parts of the season. On occasions they gather in such large numbers that they give the appearance of small smoke clouds over the water or the nearby vegetation. It must be remembered that although we see and talk about these flies as being black, very few creatures do not have some form of hue in their colouration – so black may be blue-black, brown-black, red-black and so on. The wings themselves, even though they may be described as clear, will show some tinge of colour and it does not hurt to remember this when tying artificials.

Dressings

1. Black Gnat (Roberts)

DRESSING

Hook length: Up to 8mm
Thread: Black
Abdomen: Black thread or polypropylene yarn
Wing: Pale grey yarn tied over abdomen
Hackle: Black cock

2. Black Gnat

DRESSING

Hook length: Up to 8mm
Thread: Black
Tails: Black cock fibres
Abdomen: Black fur
Wing: Grey starling
Hackle: Black cock

3. Black Pensioner (Mackenzie-Philps)

DRESSING

Hook length: Up to 8mm
Thread: Black
Tail: Black cock fibres
Abdomen: Black cock pheasant tail fibres
Rib: Gold wire
Wing: White mink hair
Hackle: Black cock tied in parachute style

4. Black Gnat

DRESSING

Hook length: Up to 8mm
Thread: Black
Abdomen: Black, slight bulge at thorax
Rib: Fine silver wire
Wing: Dull brown feather tips over abdomen
Hackle: Dark brown cock

5. Black Gnat (O'Reilly)

DRESSING

Hook length: Up to 8mm
Thread: Black
Abdomen: Bronze peacock herl
Tag: Silver tinsel
Hackle: Black cock

Plate 39

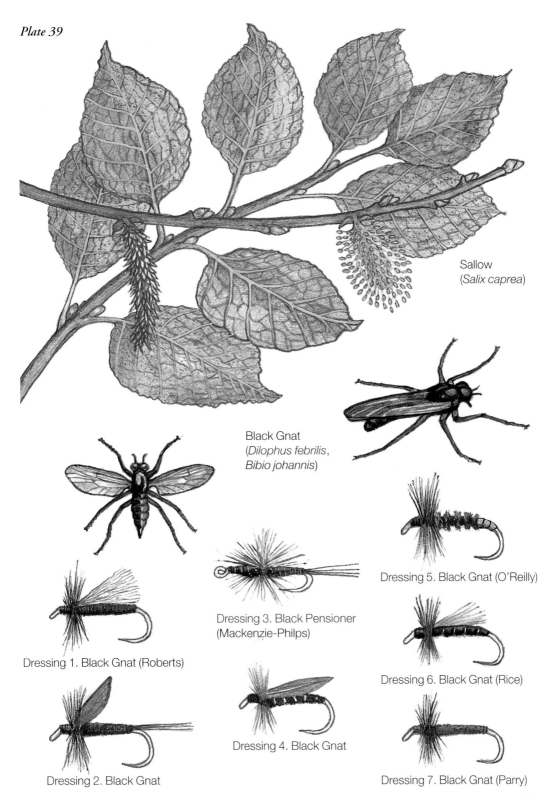

Sallow
(*Salix caprea*)

Black Gnat
(*Dilophus febrilis*,
Bibio johannis)

Dressing 5. Black Gnat (O'Reilly)

Dressing 3. Black Pensioner
(Mackenzie-Philps)

Dressing 1. Black Gnat (Roberts)

Dressing 6. Black Gnat (Rice)

Dressing 2. Black Gnat

Dressing 4. Black Gnat

Dressing 7. Black Gnat (Parry)

6. Black Gnat (Rice)

DRESSING

Hook length: Up to 8mm
Thread: Black
Abdomen: Tying thread
Rib: Silver wire
Wing: Pale blue dun fibres over abdomen
Hackle: Black cock

7. Black Gnat (Parry)

DRESSING

Hook length: Up to 8mm
Thread: Black
Abdomen: Grey floss silk
Hackle: Black cock

Sallow
Goat Willow, Pussy Willow
Salix caprea (Plate 39)

Flower head: Numerous small flowers in the form of catkins. Male catkins, 3cm long, are grey in colour but change to yellow with pollen as they open. Female catkins, 5–6cm long, are grey turning greenish-white and then develop into fluffy white seedheads

Leaves: Alternate leaves that are grey-green in colour and often twisted, may vary in size, shape and toothing. They are short-stalked and woolly beneath

Flowering time: Early spring
Height: Up to 15m
Habit: Native
Habitat: Damp woodlands, scrub, hedgerows and wet areas
Distribution: Common throughout
General: Sallow provides the familiar 'pussy willow' catkins that are gathered on Palm Sunday to decorate churches; it is the yellow male catkins that are used, even though it is the smooth silky surface of the female catkins that give rise to the name. The other common name, 'goat willow', comes from the tree's ability to survive on very poor rough ground, the kind of ground where goats were often kept. Sallow has a very soft wood and was used for making such things as hatchet handles and clothes pegs

Bluebottle
Calliphora vomitoria

Greenbottle
Luicili

Cluster-Fly
Pollenia rudis
(Plate 40)

Although there are many similar flies in shape, colour and size these three, along with the yellow-dung fly, would cover any of this type or colour of fly likely to be found on the water. *C. vomitoria* is the common bluebottle that lays its eggs on any type of meat. The eggs hatch out into the well-known coarse fisherman's friend, the maggot. The greenbottle follows a similar lifestyle to the bluebottle seeking out decaying animals on which to lay its eggs. The cluster-fly parisitises earthworms and can often be found in groups, hence the name. Although they are not one of the more common flies to be found on the water, patterns do exist and a fairly fat fly in the correct colour can prove the undoing of trout, especially under the shade of overhanging vegetation.

Dressings
1. Blue Bottle (Price)

DRESSING

Hook length: 10mm
Thread: Black
Abdomen: Blue lurex
Rib: Black ostrich herl
Wing: Blue dun hackle tips over abdomen
Hackle: Black cock

2. Housefly (Russell)

DRESSING

Hook length: 10mm
Thread: Black
Abdomen: Bronze peacock tied to shape
Wing: Two grey feathers over abdomen
Hackle: Black cock

3. Blue Bottle

DRESSING

Hook length: 10mm
Thread: Dark blue
Abdomen: Magpie herl
Rib: Thin, clear PVC or similar
Wing: Traun stonefly wing or similar
Hackle: Black cock

4. Grayling Bug (Sawyer)

DRESSING

Hook length: 15mm curved
Thread: Copper wire
Abdomen: Beige darning wool
Rib: Copper wire to give segmented effect

5. Maggot (USA)

DRESSING

Hook length: 15mm curved
Thread: White or cream
Abdomen: White or cream chenille
Rib: White swannundaze

Cowslip
Primula veris (Plate 40)
Primrose family (*Primulacaea*)

Flower head:	Numerous drooping yellow flowers carried in loose flower heads at the top of erect leafless stalks. Flowers consist of five yellow petals, each with an orange spot at the base and pale green sepals forming a bell-shaped calyx
Leaves:	More or less oval in shape, the leaves grow in basal rosettes and have fine hairs on both sides. They are wrinkled in appearance and have toothed margins
Flowering time:	April–May
Height:	10–25cm
Habit:	Native perennial
Habitat:	Meadows and grassland
Distribution:	Widespread but can be localized
General:	*Primula*, taken from the Latin word *primus* (first), true to its name is one of the first flowers to appear in spring. However, the distribution of this tufted, downy perennial has been much reduced by the destruction of grassland. It is often found growing alongside primroses with which it hybridizes to produce the false oxlip. The delicately perfumed flowers are used in winemaking and an infusion may be made with the leaves. In Somerset it was believed that the first cowslip sprang up on the spot where St Peter had dropped the keys to heaven, and so it is known locally as 'bunch of keys'

Plate 40

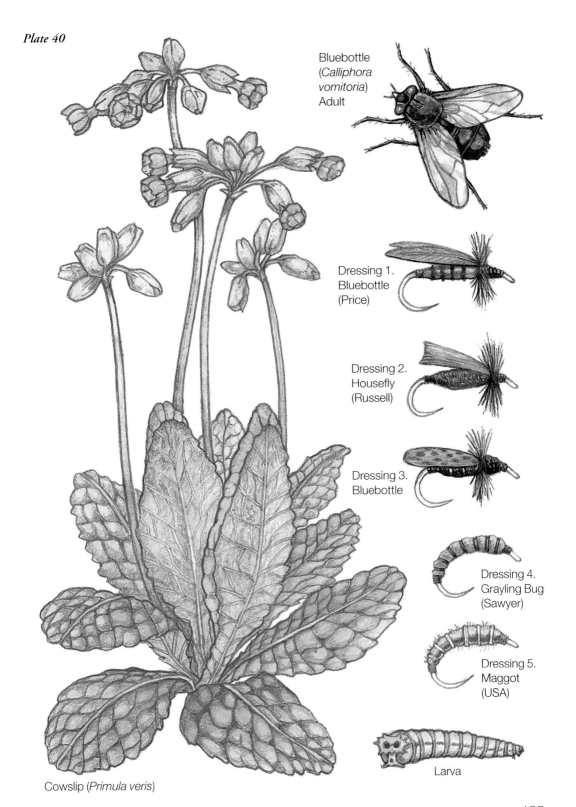

Bluebottle
(*Calliphora
vomitoria*)
Adult

Dressing 1.
Bluebottle
(Price)

Dressing 2.
Housefly
(Russell)

Dressing 3.
Bluebottle

Dressing 4.
Grayling Bug
(Sawyer)

Dressing 5.
Maggot
(USA)

Larva

Cowslip (*Primula veris*)

Cowdung Fly
Scathophaga stercoraria
(Plate 41)

Walk through any field that has had cows in and these flies will be there in numbers. Every cow-pat will have its visitors, laying their eggs in the dung, or searching for the smaller insects on which they prey. The male is the brighter yellow of the species and also greater in numbers; the female being a more drab grey-brown in colour. From the numbers that are disturbed when walking through the fields by the side of the river, it must follow that occasionally casualties must end up on the water itself and so become food for the trout. Some of the patterns to represent them have been around for a long time – dressing no. 4 is from the nineteenth-century angling entomologist, Alfred Ronalds.

Dressings

1. Cowdung Fly

DRESSING

Hook length: 10mm
Thread: Red
Abdomen: Ginger-yellow dubbing
Rib: Fine silver tinsel
Wings: Two ginger hackle tips tied over abdomen
Hackle: Ginger cock

2. Cowdung Fly (Veniard)

DRESSING

Hook length: 10mm
Thread: Yellow
Abdomen: Snuff-coloured wool or seal's fur sub
Wing: Landrail feather
Hackle: Dark ginger cock

3. Cowdung Fly (Roberts)

DRESSING

Hook length: 10mm
Thread: Yellow
Abdomen: Yellow and olive seal's fur sub
Wing: Cinnamon hen feather fibres tied over abdomen
Hackle: Pale ginger cock

4. Cowdung Fly (Ronalds)

DRESSING

Hook length: 10mm
Thread: Yellow-brown
Abdomen: Olive-coloured chenille
Rib: Pale green thread
Wing: Honey dun hackle tips
Hackle: Dark honey dun throat hackle

5. Cowdung Fly (Price)

DRESSING

Hook length: 10mm
Thread: Yellow
Abdomen: Yellow and olive seal's fur sub
Wing: Cinnamon hen wing over abdomen
Hackle: Pale ginger throat hackle

Plate 41

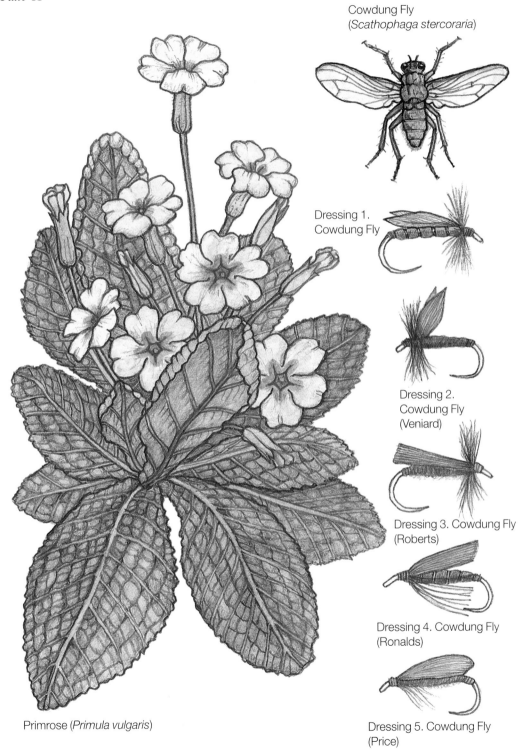

Cowdung Fly
(*Scathophaga stercoraria*)

Dressing 1.
Cowdung Fly

Dressing 2.
Cowdung Fly
(Veniard)

Dressing 3. Cowdung Fly
(Roberts)

Dressing 4. Cowdung Fly
(Ronalds)

Primrose (*Primula vulgaris*)

Dressing 5. Cowdung Fly
(Price)

Primrose
Prima Rosa, First Rose
Primula vulgaris (Plate 41)
Primrose family (*Primulaecae*)

Flower head: Single yellow flowers, 20–40mm across, are carried at the end of a short, hairy stem arising from the base. Each flower has a dark centre with light green sepals that form a bell-shaped tube

Leaves: The spoon-shaped leaves, which taper into a winged stalk, are wrinkled in appearance and have a light covering of short hairs underneath

Flowering time: March–May

Height: Up to 15cm

Habit: Native perennial

Habitat: Woodlands, meadows, damp banks and old pastures

Distribution: Common throughout

General: The primrose, prima rosa or first rose, as its names suggest, is one of the first flowers of spring and as such is one of our best-loved flowers. Although still a common sight throughout, it is much less abundant nowadays due to overpicking. It is often found growing with cowslips with which it will readily hybridize to give the false oxslip. Like other members of the primrose family, it produces two kinds of flower that can only be fertilized when the pollen from one kind is transferred to the other. In the past it was used in herbalism as a cure for gout, rheumatism and nervous headaches. A preparation made from the flowers was also an ingredient in love potions

Grasshoppers
Acrididae

Lacewings
Planipennia
(Plate 42)

Grasshoppers are usually to be found in the warmer summer months amongst the grasses on which they feed. They live for only a few months, dying off when the colder weather starts in late September. With modern farming methods their numbers have drastically reduced and so the artificial is of less importance than it once must have been. The natural is a fairly bulky insect with very strong rear legs and obvious wingcases. The normal colours are greens and browns.

Lacewings, as their name suggests, are very delicate insects and are reasonably common throughout the warmer summer months. They are a common sight in gardens and a friend to the gardener, feeding as they do in both adult and larval form on smaller insects, particularly the aphid or greenfly. A brown form also exists and this too is widely distributed. Their use to the fisherman is questionable although some patterns do exist.

Dressings

1. Brown Lacewing

DRESSING

Hook length: Up to 15mm
Thread: Brown
Abdomen: Brown floss silk
Wings: Pale blue dun hackle tips tied over abdomen
Hackle: Short pale brown cock

2. Green Lacewing

DRESSING

Hook length: Up to 15mm
Thread: Green
Abdomen: Green floss silk
Wings: Pale blue dun hackle tips tied over abdomen
Hackle: Short green cock

3. Dave's Hopper (Whitlock)

DRESSING

Hook length: Up to 20mm
Thread: Brown
Abdomen: Yellow wool
Rib: Brown hackle, palmered and trimmed
Wing case: White-tipped turkey over abdomen
Hackle: Brown deer hair
Legs: Knotted pheasant tail fibres
Head: Olive deer hair, muddler style
A bright red tail is added

4. Joe's Hopper (Winnie)

DRESSING

Hook length: Up to 20mm
Thread: Brown
Abdomen: Yellow deer hair clipped to shape
Wing case: White tipped turkey over abdomen
Hackle: Grizzle and brown wound together
A red feather fibre tail is added

5. Troth's Hopper (Troth)

DRESSING

Hook length: Up to 20mm
Thread: Olive-green
Abdomen: Olive elk hair
Wing: Green quill slip cut to shape over top of abdomen
Head andtrailing legs: Olive deer hair muddler style, some lower rear-facing fibres left to form legs

Wych Elm
Ulmus glabra (Plate 42)

Flower head: Before any foliage emerges, dense clusters of insignificant looking, dark purplish-red flowers appear close to the twigs

Leaves: Alternate leaves with double-toothed margins, 15cm long, are carried on short, stout stalks. Dark green above and paler beneath, they have hairs on both sides. The midrib is stout with veins branching off to the larger teeth

Flowering time: Early spring
Height: Up to 30m
Habit: Native
Habitat: Frequently by water and often in hilly country
Distribution: Mainly western and northern Britain
General: The wych elm is the hardiest of Britain's elms. *Wych* is an Anglo-Saxon word meaning pliable and refers to the ease with which the twigs are bent without snapping. The grey bark has long, shallow fissures. The wood is tough and very durable and has long been used for boat keels and other harbour works. At one time whole trees were hollowed out and used as water pipes. The seeds are larger than those of other elms, and the means of propagation. This is probably why it has more resistance to Dutch elm disease, as other species propagate by offshoots from their roots

Plate 42

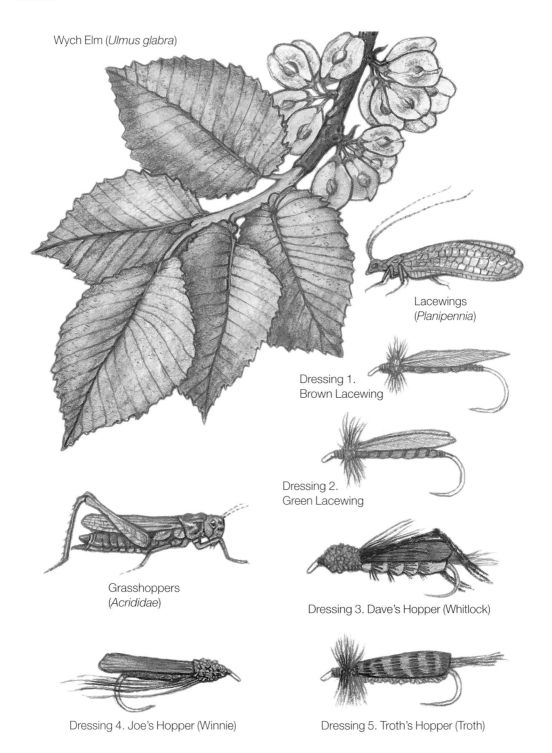

Wych Elm (*Ulmus glabra*)

Lacewings
(*Planipennia*)

Dressing 1.
Brown Lacewing

Dressing 2.
Green Lacewing

Grasshoppers
(*Acrididae*)

Dressing 3. Dave's Hopper (Whitlock)

Dressing 4. Joe's Hopper (Winnie)

Dressing 5. Troth's Hopper (Troth)

Gravel Bed
Hexatoma fuscipennis
(Plate 43)

This is similar to the crane-fly, the overall colour being a dark greyish-brown with well-marked wings and a long, thin pointed abdomen. One of the reasons why it is of interest to the fisherman is because the eggs, larvae and pupae are to be found in damp ground close to rivers with a gravely base. These rivers are usually upland streams and so, although common where it occurs, this fly is limited in its distribution. Its habit of flying low over the water surface makes it vulnerable to the trout.

Dressings

1. Gravel Bed (Fogg)

DRESSING

Hook length: 11mm
Thread: Dark grey
Abdomen: Tying thread
Thorax: Mole's fur
Hackle: Dark brown or slate-coloured cock tied in parachute style

2. Gravel Bed (Veniard)

DRESSING

Hook length: 11mm
Thread: Lead-coloured silk
Wing: Woodcock wing feather
Hackle: Black cock

3. Clyde Sandfly

DRESSING

Hook length: 11mm
Thread: Black
Abdomen: Black thread
Wing: Hen pheasant tail
Hackle: Black cock long in the fibre

4. Gravel Bed

DRESSING

Hook length: 11mm
Thread: Brown
Abdomen: Brown thread
Thorax: Fine brown dubbing
Wing: Feather fibres 'V' shaped over abdomen
Hackle: Dull brown cock

5. Partridge and Blue

DRESSING

Hook length: 11mm
Thread: Blue
Abdomen: Tying thread lightly dubbed with fine lead-coloured wool
Hackle: Brown partridge

Plate 43

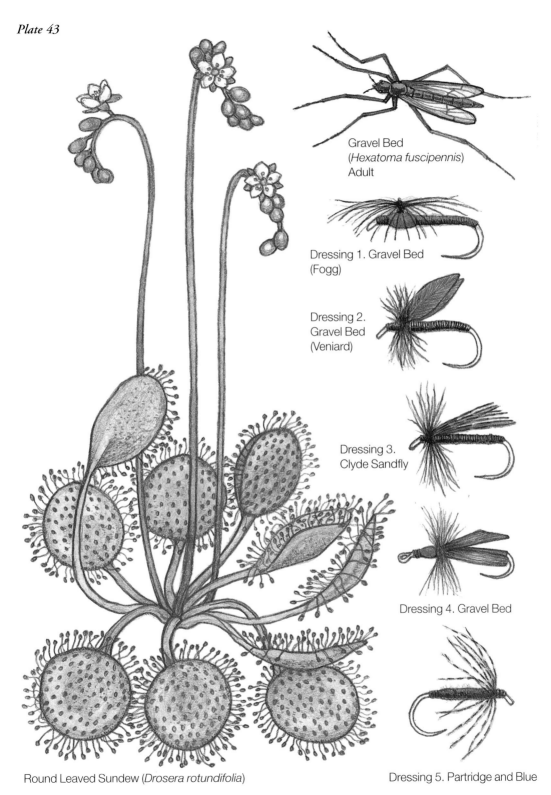

Gravel Bed
(*Hexatoma fuscipennis*)
Adult

Dressing 1. Gravel Bed
(Fogg)

Dressing 2.
Gravel Bed
(Veniard)

Dressing 3.
Clyde Sandfly

Dressing 4. Gravel Bed

Round Leaved Sundew (*Drosera rotundifolia*)

Dressing 5. Partridge and Blue

Round Leaved Sundew
Drosera rotundifolia (Plate 43)
Sundew family (*Droseraceae*)

Flower head: Clusters of tiny white or pink flowers carried in a spike at the end of a leafless flower stalk. Each flower has five or six pointed white petals and an equal number of green sepals

Leaves: A basal rosette of round, fleshy leaves that are covered in tiny red glands. Each leaf is borne at the end of a long stalk

Flowering time: June–August

Height: Up to 20cm

Habit: Perennial

Habitat: Wet moorland, marsh and boggy land

Distribution: Common

General: This is the most common of Britain's three native sundews. It is a carnivorous plant, trapping and digesting insects by means of its specialized leaves. Glands on the leaves secrete a substance that insects adhere to, hairs on the leaves then bend to trap the insects even more. Whilst trapped, they are digested by the chemicals secreted from the glands and any nutrients produced as a result are absorbed into the leaves. In this way the plant helps to make up for any mineral deficiencies in its habitat

Greenfly
Blackfly
Aphids (Plate 44)

These are some of the worst pests in the garden, occurring in large numbers during the growing season. Not only do they live on garden plants, they will live on grasses, trees or any new growth that is to their liking. In some years immense numbers can be found and at these times, coupled with breezy conditions, many can end up on the water surface. In back eddies, under trees, you will often see fish swimming around smutting at the surface film, at these times it is well worth trying something green or black in very small sizes. The aphid is a fairly easy fly to copy with a basic bulbous abdomen, coupled with a small hackle. Remember that the natural may only be up to about 3mm so the corresponding artificial should be of a similar size, but as fish take these insects in great numbers you should always carry a copy in the fly-box. The greenfly can also be a useful grayling fly – when autumn arrives and the leaves start to fall, any residual members of the colony are carried on to the water with the leaves. So if you ever see fish active amongst leaf litter on the surface, once again the greenfly is worth a try.

Dressings

1. Greenfly

> **DRESSING**
>
> **Hook length:** 4mm
> **Thread:** Green
> **Abdomen:** Tying thread built up to shape
> **Hackle:** White

2. Arrow Fly (Courtney Williams)

> **DRESSING**
>
> **Hook length:** Up to 10mm (in large size represents a group of aphis or caterpillar)
> **Thread:** Green
> **Abdomen:** Emerald-green thread
> **Hackle:** Palmered short white cock

3. Green Midge

> **DRESSING**
>
> **Hook length:** 4mm
> **Thread:** Green
> **Abdomen:** Fine green wool
> **Hackle:** White cock

4. Black Midge (Walker)

> **DRESSING**
>
> **Hook length:** 4mm
> **Thread:** Black
> **Abdomen:** Fine feather fibres
> **Wing:** Very short white hackle tips
> **Hackle:** Short black cock

5. Green Insect

> **DRESSING**
>
> **Hook length:** 5mm
> **Thread:** Green
> **Abdomen:** Green peacock herl
> **Tag:** Red silk
> **Hackle:** Blue dun cock

6. Aphis

DRESSING

Hook length: 5mm
Thread: Green
Abdomen: Green peacock herl
Wing: White DRF tied flat over abdomen
Hackle: Dyed green cock

Bluebell
Wild Hyacinth
Hyacinthoides-non scripta
(Plate 44)
Lily family (*Liliacae*)

Flower head: Numerous small bell-shaped flowers carried on a spike that curves at the tip. The blue, sometimes white or pink, blossoms have recurved petals, yellow anthers and are richly scented

Leaves: A rosette of narrow, somewhat fleshy leaves, which are 'V' shaped in cross-section

Flowering time: May–June
Height: 20–50cm
Habit: Native perennial
Habitat: Woodland and shady habitats
Distribution: Common throughout England and Scotland
General: *Hyacinthoides*, as its name suggests, resembles another much-loved flower, the hyacinth. This popular perennial is a very common sight during springtime when it grows in vast, scented patches in woodlands and other shady places. The large, fleshy bulb is a food store of sugars and starches. At one time it was a source for a starch-based glue used in bookbinding, and also for stiffening collars and ruffs in Elizabethan times. Picking the flowers does no harm to the plant as was once thought, but crushing the leaves in the process deprives the plant of its food and is probably what has caused it to be less prevalent nowadays

Plate 44

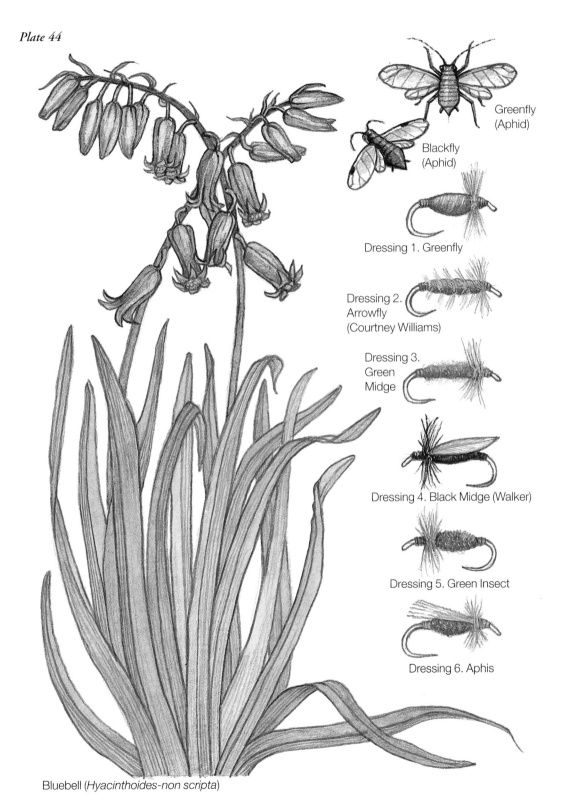

Greenfly
(Aphid)

Blackfly
(Aphid)

Dressing 1. Greenfly

Dressing 2.
Arrowfly
(Courtney Williams)

Dressing 3.
Green
Midge

Dressing 4. Black Midge (Walker)

Dressing 5. Green Insect

Dressing 6. Aphis

Bluebell (*Hyacinthoides-non scripta*)

Hawthorn Fly St Mark's Fly
Bibio Marci (Plate 45)

This is one of the earliest terrestrial flies to be of interest to the fisherman and when conditions are right it can cause quite a stir amongst the trout. It is sometimes referred to as 'St Mark's fly', St Mark's day being on 25 April, around the time when the fly puts in its first appearance. It is a very short season fly, the flight period being over in just two or three weeks in early May. This is the time when the hawthorn blossom is out and large numbers may be seen around the hawthorn bushes, hence its other common name. The fly is black with a large, hairy thorax and transparent wings with black leading edges. The most obvious means of identification in flight are the long, trailing legs that are included as a part of the design of most artificials. The adult is up to 13mm in length.

Dressings

1. Hawthorn Fly (Price)

DRESSING

Hook length: Up to 13mm
Thread: Black
Abdomen: Black pheasant tail fibres
Wing: White hackle tips
Hackle: Black cock
Legs: Black pheasant tail fibres, knotted

2. Hawthorn Fly (Beer)

DRESSING

Hook length: Up to 13mm
Thread: Black
Abdomen: Black deer hair tied in along hook shank, butts at the eye then wrapped with tying thread
Wings: Vinyl repair patch cut to shape and tied in over abdomen
Hackle: Black cock
Legs: Knotted black hackle stalks

3. Hawthorn Fly (Warrilow)

DRESSING

Hook length: Up to 13mm
Thread: Black
Abdomen: Black pheasant tail fibres
Wing: Traun stonefly wing
Hackle: Black cock
Legs: Knotted black pheasant tail fibres

Hawthorn
Maytree, Quickthorn
Crataegus monogyna (Plate 45)

Flower head:	Dense bunches of sixteen or more white flowers each 1–5cm across with pink anthers
Leaves:	Shiny, dark green leaves, 5–7cm long, with coarsely toothed, irregular lobes and two leafy bracts at the base of the short stalk. Leaves have pink veining beneath
Flowering time:	May
Height:	Up to 15m
Habit:	Native
Habitat:	Various
Distribution:	Common throughout

Plate 45

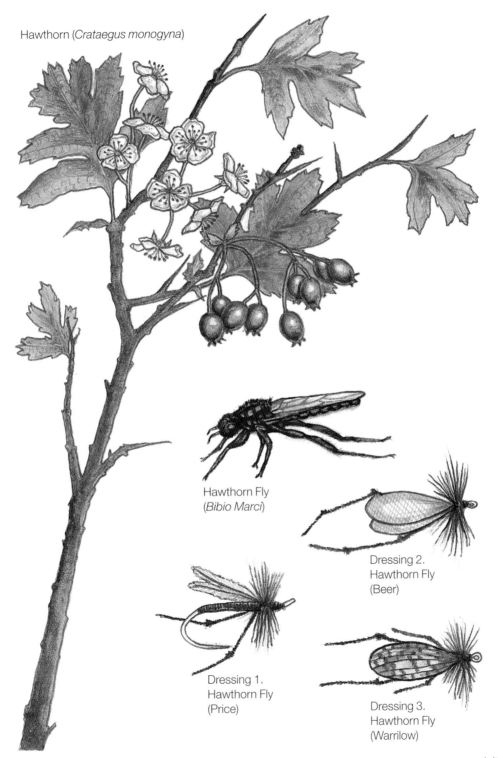

Hawthorn (*Crataegus monogyna*)

Hawthorn Fly
(*Bibio Marci*)

Dressing 1.
Hawthorn Fly
(Price)

Dressing 2.
Hawthorn Fly
(Beer)

Dressing 3.
Hawthorn Fly
(Warrilow)

General: A full-grown hawthorn tree in May covered with masses of snow-white flowers and filling the air with its sweet, sickly smell is a familiar sight to everyone. It is also a familiar sight in the autumn when the flowers are replaced by clusters of rich red berries or haws. Hawthorns have been a common sight since the land enclosures of the seventeenth and eighteenth centuries as they have been widely used for hedging. With their straight, sharp thorns and dense nature when cut regularly they are ideal for forming a strong, impenetrable barrier. The young leaves, which have a nutty flavour, were known in some parts of the country as 'bread and cheese'. The Glastonbury thorn (*C. biflora*), which allegedly took root when Joseph of Arimathea planted his staff in the ground at Glastonbury, is a variety of hawthorn. According to folklore, destroying hawthorn is to invite disaster upon oneself

Heather Fly
Bibio pomonae (Plate 46)

Like the hawthorn fly, this fly is associated with the plant that it is named after. It is more commonly found in Scotland, the north of England and parts of Wales. Although similar and related to the hawthorn fly, it is easily identified by its bright red thighs. It is to be found later in the season, towards the end of July through to September. On windy days it can be blown on to the surface of lochs and still waters in large numbers, providing a feast for the trout. The adult is up to 13mm long. All the patterns designed to cover the hawthorn fly can be adjusted to copy the heather fly.

Dressings

1. Heather Fly (Price)

> **DRESSING**
>
> **Hook length:** Up to 13mm
> **Thread:** Black
> **Abdomen:** Black rayon floss
> **Rib:** Silver wire
> **Wing:** Grey duck's feather over abdomen
> **Hackle:** Dyed red cock
> **Legs:** Knotted black pheasant tail fibres

2. Heather Fly (Jardine)

> **DRESSING**
>
> **Hook length:** Up to 13mm
> **Thread:** Black
> **Abdomen:** Dark peacock herl
> **Rib:** Silver wire
> **Wing:** Two blue dun hackle tips
> **Hackle:** Dyed red cock
> **Legs:** Knotted black swan fibres

3. Heather Fly (Warrilow)

> **DRESSING**
>
> **Hook length:** Up to 13mm
> **Thread:** Black
> **Abdomen:** Black pheasant tail fibres
> **Wing:** Traun stonefly wing
> **Hackle:** Dyed red cock
> **Legs:** Knotted black pheasant tail fibres

4. Heather Fly

> **DRESSING**
>
> **Hook length:** Up to 13mm
> **Thread:** Black
> **Abdomen:** Black ostrich herl
> **Hackle:** Coch-y-bonddu cock

Heather
Ling
Calluna vulgaris (Plate 46)
Heather family (*Ericaceae*)

Flower head:	Tiny bell-shaped flowers, 2–4mm long, in loose spikes at the ends of branches. Usually pink to purplish-red in colour, they may also be lilac or white
Leaves:	Tiny evergreen leaves which are somewhat stiff and stalkless
Flowering time:	July–September
Height:	20–60cm
Habit:	Native shrub
Habitat:	Heaths, moors, bogs and woodland banks in acid soil
Distribution:	Common throughout

General: An easily recognizable evergreen shrub on moors and heaths where it forms huge patches of colour during the summer months. It is a rather straggly looking plant due to its many branched and tangled stems. Heather is a very important plant on grouse moors where it is regularly burnt to prevent it from becoming too woody. The tender young shoots form an important part of the grouse's diet and the flowers are a valuable source of nectar for bees. In the past some of its many uses included bedding, thatching and basketry, but most important of all was its usefulness as a fuel when dried

Plate 46

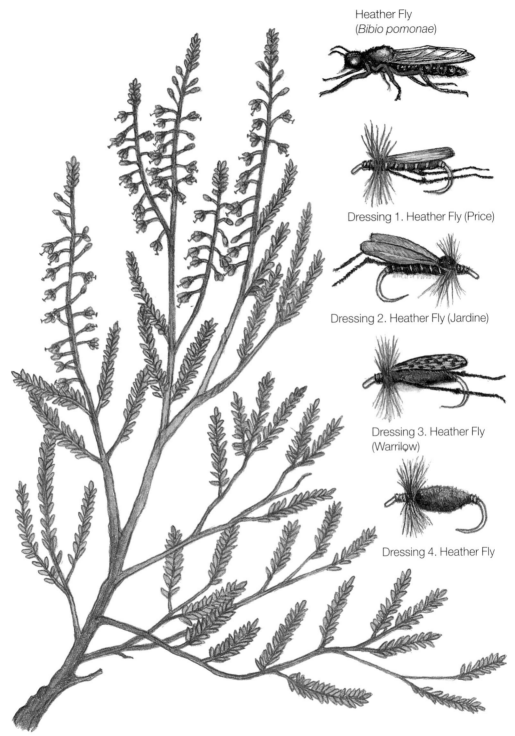

Heather Fly
(*Bibio pomonae*)

Dressing 1. Heather Fly (Price)

Dressing 2. Heather Fly (Jardine)

Dressing 3. Heather Fly
(Warrilow)

Dressing 4. Heather Fly

Heather (*Calluna vulgaris*)

PART 4

Life Cycles

Points of particular interest
in the life cycles of food forms to the trout
and therefore the trout fisherman

Most of the food forms available to the trout go through some form of metamorphosis. The different stages of change make the various creatures at times easily accessible and at others of no interest to the trout. It is the points in the life cycle that make the food forms available that the flytier-fisherman must concentrate upon, the design and fishing of the fly mirroring these stages.

In the case of stoneflies the life cycle is egg, nymph, adult, mating, female egg laying, spent female. Of these stages, the insect would only be available to the trout in the nymph, egg-laying female and spent female forms. Neither the egg, nor the emerging and mating adults would be of interest because this takes place on stones or vegetation near to the water. So, although there may be slight variations, only three main stages in the life cycle of the stonefly are of relevance for flytying.

In comparison, the life cycle of upwinged flies has the following stages: egg, nymph, dun, spinner, mating, egg-laying female, spent fly. Of these stages, the nymph, emerger, dun, spinner and spent female

(male) would all be available to the trout and therefore of interest to the fisherman.

The following detailed drawings and explanatory text will, I hope, be useful as patterns to show why many of the existing designs of fly work, and of help in the creation of new designs. It must, of course, be remembered that drawings are two-dimensional and lifeless, the flytyer however must work in three dimensions and introduce the illusion of life. It will become obvious by the study of the following illustrations that some food forms are a great deal more difficult to copy than others and require many more 'stages' of patterns.

However, it must also be remembered that although we can make fly-fishing as detailed and complex as we wish, it must always be enjoyable, and if you wish to keep things simple then by all means do so. I have stated many times that you could still catch fish with just the following three patterns of fly in different sizes – dry, emerger and nymph. But if you have enough time on your hands and wish to either copy or create, then I hope the drawings are of use.

Upwinged Flies
(Plate 47)

The illustration shows the stages in the metamorphosis of the upwinged fly. The first stage of interest to the fish and fisherman is the nymph. The body is basically the same in all species; fairly small antennae, six legs, a thorax with obvious wing buds, an abdomen with ten segments tapering towards the rear and ending in three tails. The segmented abdomen carries gills on each segment on either side of the body. The most obvious variations from family to family occur in the overall shape – some nymphs are slim, others have a broader, more flattened appearance. These variations allow them to cope with the differing habitats in which they live. Another point of relevance is the gills, which on some nymphs are small and oval and therefore not very obvious; on others they are long and feathery and much more pronounced.

When the nymph is mature and all conditions are suitable it will swim to the surface and the thorax will split to allow the adult to emerge. At this stage the fly is very vulnerable to the trout because the surface tension, coupled with the time required for the fly to break free of the nymphal schuck, gives adequate time for the trout to attack. The imitation of this stage in the life cycle must take into consideration that part of the fly is nymph and part is adult. The fly will also be very low riding in the surface of the water, not on it. The designed fly will be slim to the rear but 'fussy' at the front to allow for emerging wings, head, legs, and so on. At this point the wings are not fully emerged and therefore not dominant in the design.

When the dun has emerged from the schuck and become a fully formed adult it must take a little time before alighting from the water. Now the wings are fully formed and fairly dominant in the design, the abdomen and tails are fully extended and the feet are causing a dimpling pattern on the water surface, 'the footprint of the fly'. The dun will, if having escaped the interest of the fish, fly from the water surface and find a suitable place to moult.

Now the spinner emerges and is ready to perform its most important act – that of mating. In many of the species, mating takes place away from the water and so the male spinner dies on land. The mated female, full of eggs, returns to the water to carry out her last act. Although some species show variations in egg laying, many lay directly into the water surface and the female falls 'spent', dead, on the surface making small rings in her death throes. The spent females may not be very obvious and can be easily overlooked, so the design of fly is such that the body, tails and wings lie flat in the surface film.

The adult fly, the dun and the spinner are fairly easy to differentiate. The dun has dull colours and drab wings. The emerged spinner is much brighter. Although the same shape as the dun, it has two pairs of wings, occasionally one in a few species, and either two or three long tails. The colours can have changed considerably and the wings are shiny and clear. The male differs from the female in having larger eyes and mating claspers at the rear of the abdomen, the front legs are usually longer and are put to use in the mating flight.

Plate 47

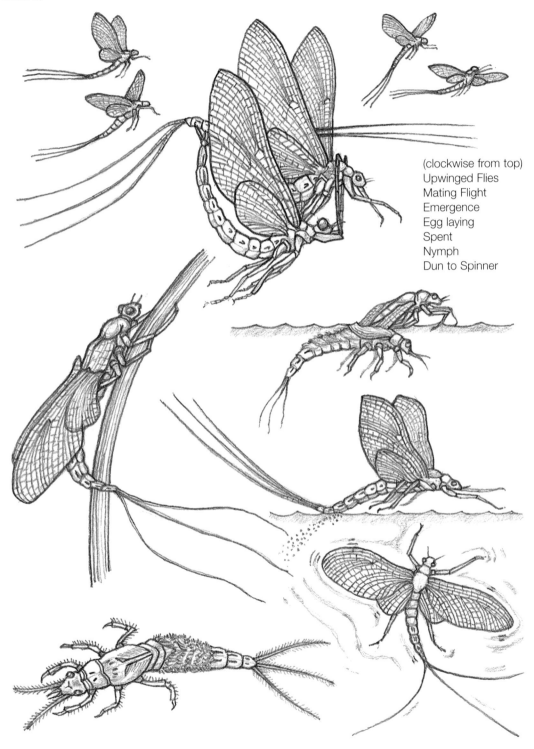

(clockwise from top)
Upwinged Flies
Mating Flight
Emergence
Egg laying
Spent
Nymph
Dun to Spinner

Sedge Flies
(Plate 48)

The illustration shows the complete metamorphosis of the sedge fly. The first stage of interest to the fish is the larva, which is different from both the stonefly and the ephemera larvae. Most sedge flies in the larval stage build a case and this becomes more important in the design of the artificial than the larva itself. Of those species that do not build a case, the larvae are termed as 'free-living'. They are generally coloured shades of green and brown, and somewhat similar to a caterpillar or grub in shape. The free-living larvae have fairly long, tapering bodies, three pairs of legs and breathing filaments down either side of the underneath of the abdomen. To avoid being swept away by the water flow, they are able to anchor themselves firmly by means of a silk thread. There are several existing patterns to represent these forms and they are reasonably easy to imitate and to fish in a natural drag-free manner.

The cased caddis represents a different tying problem in that the case itself is the prominent part of the design, with head and legs peeping out of the end. The cases can be made from any suitable material that is available. In many species, the case is long and tapered, the broader end being the opening for the head and legs. The larva spends much of its time trundling along the bottom looking for food. Extra material is added to the case as the larva grows. The artificials should take into consideration the shape of the case and the material available, as well as the species involved.

When the larvae have reached maturity, the cased or uncased caddis attach themselves to the river or lake bed. Uncased larvae now construct a case and all species pupate within the case.

Following pupation, the pupa frees itself from the case and proceeds to the surface where emergence takes place. At this point it is very vulnerable to feeding trout and many patterns have been designed to copy this stage. The pupa is made up of a segmented body, antennae, obvious wing buds, and long, trailing legs.

On reaching the surface the pupal skin splits open and the adult quickly emerges. Because of the speed of the emergence, very few adults are taken at this stage – it is more often the rising pupae that are taken avidly by the trout. The now fully formed adult leaves the water to find bankside vegetation where mating will take place. It is at this point, when the returning female flies over or touches down on the surface of the water to release her eggs, that the trout will make slashing rises at the sedge.

The adult sedge fly is very similar to a moth and there are two positions that are copied. One is the fluttering caddis where the wings are designed to show movement; the other is with the wings at rest in the familiar 'tent' shape over the abdomen. After egg laying, the adult sedge will fall 'spent' on the surface and the design of the artificial should reflect this.

Plate 48

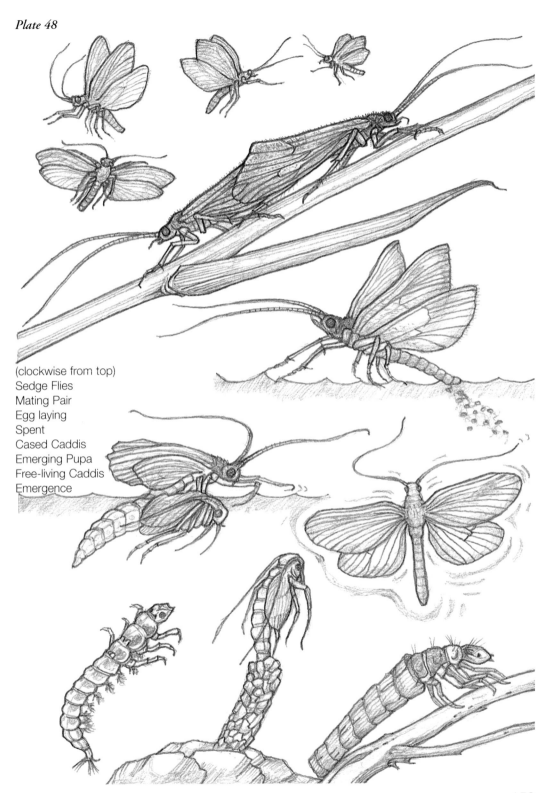

(clockwise from top)
Sedge Flies
Mating Pair
Egg laying
Spent
Cased Caddis
Emerging Pupa
Free-living Caddis
Emergence

Stoneflies
(Plate 49)

The illustration shows the stages in the metamorphosis of the stonefly. Once again, the nymph is the first stage of interest. Although in some ways similar to the upwinged nymphs, it differs in various aspects. Because stonefly nymphs, as the name implies, are usually found in fast-flowing stony rivers, they are far more robust than most upwinged nymphs. The stonefly nymph has a fairly stocky head with two obvious antennae, three pairs of strong legs, a pronounced thorax with obvious wing buds, a stout, segmented abdomen with no obvious gills, and two tails. Large variations only occur in the size of the species and colouration. The habits of the nymphs differ from the ephemera nymphs in that they are invariably bottom-crawlers. The above features must all be incorporated into the design of the nymph and in nearly all cases weight should be added to keep the artificial fishing at the correct depth.

When the nymph is mature it will leave the water to shed its nymphal schuck and emerge as an adult fly. This stage is again similar to that of the ephemera but, whereas the ephemera is now at its most vulnerable to predation, this stage of the stonefly's life cycle mostly takes place on waterside stones, away from the greedy trout. Consequently, the emerger stonefly is of no importance to the fisherman or the fish.

The emerged adult stonefly now has wings but in all other respects is very similar to the mature nymph, although in some males the wings are little better than wing buds. Stoneflies, for all their size, are very poor fliers and spend much of their time crawling about bankside stones and vegetation. When mating has taken place, the female returns to the water to lay her eggs. Because she is a poor flier, she will either flutter over the surface or rest, making quite a disturbance on the water surface, which will attract the attention of the hungry trout. Two basic designs have arisen to represent this.

The stonefly's wings are totally different from those of the ephemera in that the stonefly holds its wings flat over the body, in some cases they are even wrapped around the abdomen. They are also harder than the wings of the ephemera and darker in colouration, which should be reflected in the artificial.

After egg laying the female will die and lay spent on the surface, so the corresponding artificial will be designed to lie awash in the surface film.

Plate 49

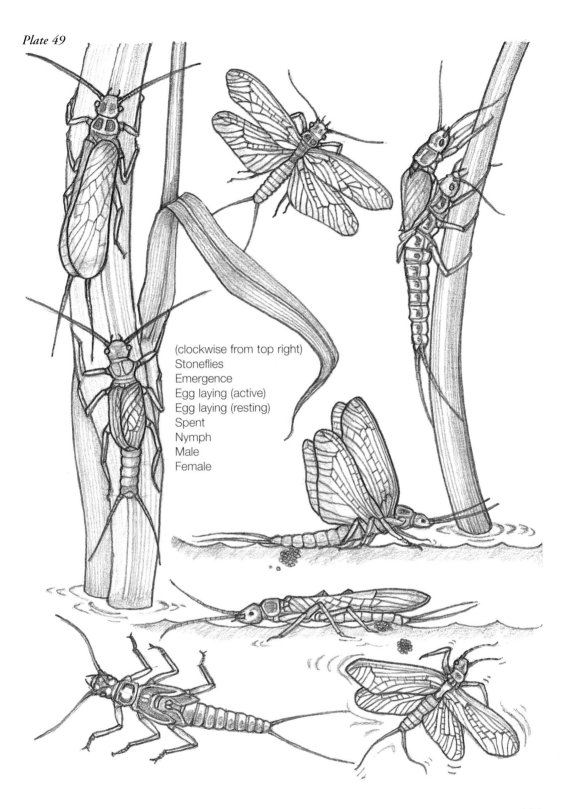

(clockwise from top right)
Stoneflies
Emergence
Egg laying (active)
Egg laying (resting)
Spent
Nymph
Male
Female

Midges
(Plate 50)

The illustration shows the metamorphosis of the aquatic midge, one of the most abundant food forms available to the trout and distributed throughout all trout waters. The first stage in the life cycle that is available to the fish and so copied by the fly-fisherman is the larva. These occur, where the environment is suitable, in vast numbers and have been given the common names 'jokers' or 'bloodworms'. The term 'bloodworm' is to some extent misleading for only some forms have the red colouration, whilst others are shades of green, brown and yellow. The basic shape is thin and worm-like with a segmented body and the artificial should reflect this. The larva is very flexible but poor at moving through the water using a looping motion. The artificial should preferably be weighted and fished mid-water or near the bottom.

Many species live in the soft mud and debris on the river or lake bed. When fully grown and conditions are right, the larva begins to pupate and this brings dramatic changes in the structure of the creature. The abdomen area swells and the formation of legs and wing buds can be clearly seen. Some pupae have feathery gills on the top of the head, whilst others have horn-like appendages. In all pupae of the various flat-winged flies the basic shape of the artificial is similar and the main differences will be of colouration. A few sizes tied in various colours will cover most fishing requirements. Some artificials will be tied weighted to fish at depth but as the pupa is at its most vulnerable when in the surface film, a lot of artificials are fished just below or in the surface.

Once the pupa arrives at the surface, the skin behind the head and thorax splits to allow the emergence of the adult. The adult escapes the pupal skin at various speeds depending on weather conditions. In warm, dry conditions the adult will escape very quickly. Like the pupae, most adults have the same basic shape – a long, slim abdomen extending beyond the length of the wings, one pair of wings held flat over the abdomen when at rest and three pairs of fairly long, thin, splayed-out legs. The male plumed midge has, as the name suggests, very obvious feathery antennae. However, the difference between species is generally one of colour and size, the colours ranging from orange-brown to olive, black, grey and green.

The adult males will gather together to form mating swarms that at times appear like small clouds under trees and similar places. Once mating has taken place the female returns to the water to lay her eggs where she will again become vulnerable to the trout.

Plate 50

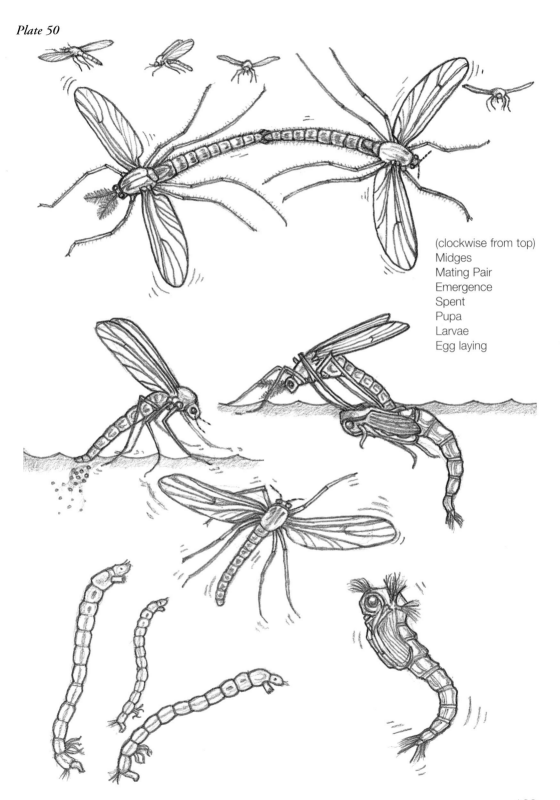

(clockwise from top)
Midges
Mating Pair
Emergence
Spent
Pupa
Larvae
Egg laying

Damselflies and Dragonflies

(Plate 51)

The illustration shows the stages in the metamorphosis of the damsel and dragonflies. These two insects are so similar in many ways that they can be linked together for fishing purposes with most emphasis being placed on the damselfly because of its size and availability to fish.

The nymph is the first stage of interest to the fisherman. It is a large creature when compared with nymphs of most insect species and fiercely carnivorous, feeding on most aquatic invertebrates, even taking tadpoles and small fish. The nymph is made up of a large, segmented abdomen that is slightly flattened, fairly long legs, small tails in the case of damselflies, and no obvious gills. All species have a fairly complex head containing an extendable 'mask' with a pair of pincers for seizing their prey. Some species also have very pronounced eyes taking up a large section of the head. The wing buds are also obvious. Colours of the nymphs vary but are mostly brown or green. Damselfly nymphs are strong swimmers and move with an undulating motion. The corresponding artificial is usually fished with some form of weight and because of the swimming action of the natural, movement is given to the retrieve.

When the nymph is fully developed it will leave the water and moulting into the adult will take place. This follows the usual procedure with the top of the thorax splitting open to allow the adult to emerge. At this stage the newly emerged insect does not have the full colours of the sexually mature adult, which may take up to three weeks to occur. Because of the nature of the emergence, the fly at this stage is not available to the trout and so no emerger patterns exist. The adults are also carnivorous, hunting by sight using their huge eyes to target the prey and capture it in flight. Before and after mating, the pair may fly in tandem and even stay in this position with the male helping to hold the female whilst she deposits her eggs in the stems of plants below the water level. Some species drop their eggs into the water surface. Adults become available to trout either when egg laying or as windborne casualties.

The pattern is a long, slender body with a built-up thorax, a hackle to represent legs and two long, slender wings tied over the abdomen. In the spent position, two pairs of wings are tied in a splayed formation. The usual colours are blue-black, green and red. The artificial can be 'twitched' over the water surface or, in the case of the spent form, left undisturbed to attract a passing fish.

Plate 51

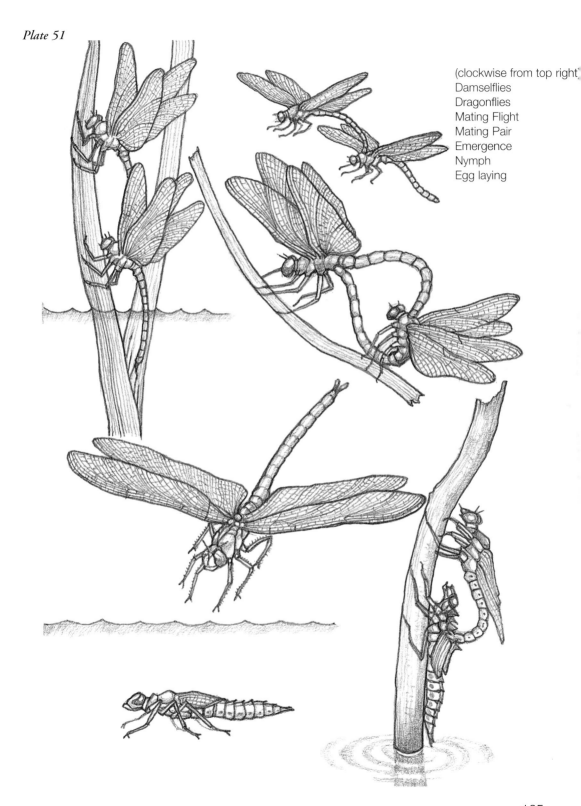

(clockwise from top right)
Damselflies
Dragonflies
Mating Flight
Mating Pair
Emergence
Nymph
Egg laying

Meniscus Midge
(Plate 52)

The larva, pupa and adult of the meniscus midge are all available to the trout. The larvae are usually to be found in shallower areas of water amongst rocks and floating vegetation. The overall attitude and shape is fairly distinctive. When at rest, the body, which is fairly uniform in width throughout its length, adopts a 'U' shape and movement is accomplished by extending alternately the two parts of the 'U'. Air is absorbed by means of spiracles on the rear end. The colour is usually a pale brown-grey with a darker tail and head. Any artificial would be reasonably easy to tie and to fish. When mature, the larva changes into the pupa and becomes very similar to other midge pupae; a segmented body, obvious head and wing buds and two breathing appendages on top of the head. All standard-type artificials would be of use, the colour being generally pale brown-grey.

The adult is similar to other midges and mosquitoes with a fairly slim abdomen and an obvious thorax. The wings extend beyond the abdomen and the antennae are fairly long and fine. The overall colour is a dark greyish-brown.

Phantom Midge
(Plate 52)

The phantom midge in the larval stage can be distinguished from other midge larvae as it is so transparent that all the internal organs are visible through the skin. Also, it does not hang in the surface film but lies horizontal to it. This is done with the help of two air sacs, one at the thorax end, and the other towards the rear. These air sacs balance the larva, allowing it to float horizontally in the water at any depth. The larva is carnivorous and catches small food items with its modified antennae. The artificial would be tied slim with an under dubbing to reflect the internal organs, two darker areas to the front and rear for the air sacs, and then the whole covered in polythene rib. The alternative would be an underbody of silver with the two darker air sacs marked and then covered with polythene. The artificial could be weighted or left to float horizontally in the surface film.

When the larva is mature it will form into the pupa. The pupa, although similar to other species, has the habit of hanging almost vertically and without the normal curve of most other pupae, although the overall shape is still basically the same. The pupa is free-swimming and can, at times, be fairly active. The abdomen is segmented with a bulbous head and thorax, obvious wing buds and two 'horns' on the top. The pupa is also semi-transparent and so the artificial should reflect this in the same manner as the larva.

The pupa, when mature, will hatch into an adult, appearing as a small, pale-coloured midge very similar to the chironomids. The difference is in the wing venation and the overall uniform colouration, which is pale green or grey-brown. Any midge pattern in a corresponding size and colour should work.

Plate 52

Meniscus Midge

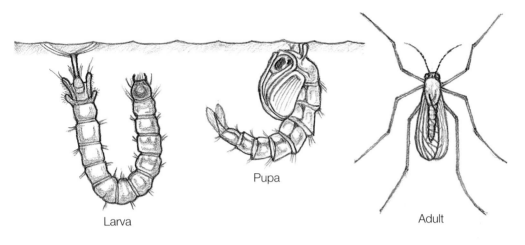

Larva

Pupa

Adult

Phantom Midge

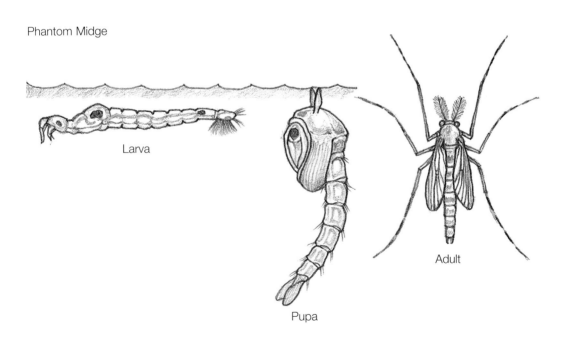

Larva

Pupa

Adult

Mosquito
(Plate 53)

The two main mosquitoes of interest to the fisherman are C. culex and C. anopheles. In both species the larvae, pupae and adults all become available to the fish. In the larval stage C. culex has a breathing tube at the tail end and adopts the position of hanging head downwards at the water surface. It is usually coloured grey to gingery-olive. C. anopheles, although very similar to C. culex, does not have the breathing tube at this stage and hangs horizontally in the surface film. The naturals are very small and this would have to be reflected in the tying of the artificial.

After moulting several times the larva develops into the pupa; both species at this stage are almost identical and being very small they would require a corresponding sized hook. The pupa is a greenish colour and is basically the standard design of any other midge pupa.

On maturity the pupa hangs in the film allowing the adult to break free. Both species are still almost impossible to tell apart – only in the resting position are they distinguishable, as is shown in the corresponding illustrations. After mating, the female will return to the water to deposit her eggs. Both species are generally a ginger-brown colour with reasonably long legs and two wings held flat over the body when at rest. The standard midge-type patterns would apply.

Plate 53

Culicine Mosquito

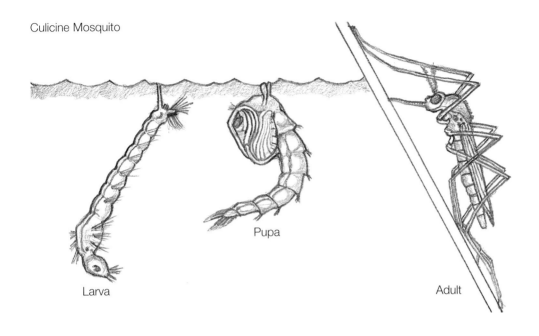

Larva

Pupa

Adult

Anopheline Mosquito

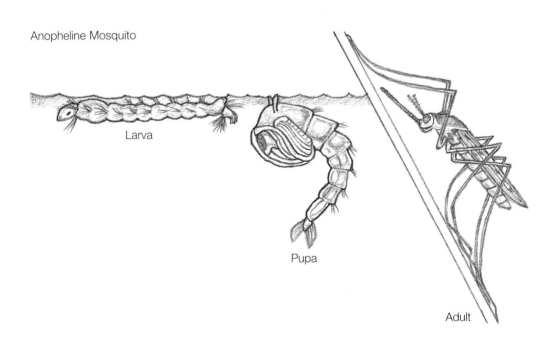

Larva

Pupa

Adult

Hover Fly
(Plate 54)

The hover, or drone fly, is very similar in appearance to some species of bee. Named because of its ability to hover in one position before darting off to repeat the movement in another location, some species are very common around garden borders and fascinating to watch.

The hover fly is available to fish in both its adult and larval forms. The larva is known by the common name of the 'rat-tailed maggot' and although mostly found in stagnant waters, several patterns have been designed to copy it and fished with some success. The basic shape is that of a maggot with a long breathing tube, its colour is creamy grey-white.

The adult fly is a rich red-brown, plump in the abdomen with a pronounced thorax and head, and two wings that are held at rest in a flat delta-winged shape. The wings beat very quickly to allow for the extremely fast controlled flight.

The artificial patterns would only be of use where obvious signs of the natural were in evidence.

Reed Smut
(Plate 54)

The reed smut is available to the trout in its larval, pupal and adult forms. The main problem with them is the small size of the natural. The larva, which has a strange club-shape, is found anchored at the base to weeds and stones. Apart from the shape the only other obvious detail is the feeding fronds on the head that are used to capture particles drifting in the water. The colour is a pale brown. Although the larva usually remains attached, if it wishes to move or is disturbed, it can do so by means of a looping action and the use of a silk safety line. A simple tying of an artificial would be possible but fishing it in a natural manner would be difficult.

Formation into the pupa takes place inside a pouch-shaped cocoon attached to stones and weeds. The pupa itself is small, stout and segmented with wing buds and two prominent respiratory filaments like fans on the head. The colour is grey-brown, darkening towards the time of emergence. A very small standard pupa pattern would copy the natural if dressed in the correct colour.

The adult reed smut, which is fully formed inside the cocoon and contained in a bubble of air, rises to the water surface. On reaching the surface it is released from the bursting bubble and quickly escapes into the air. The adult is black with a distinctly humped thorax and strongly veined wings that lie flat over the body when at rest. The artificial must be tied very small and fished on a fine leader. Fish must be given time to take the artificial and the strike just a tightening of the line to avoid breakages.

Plate 54

Reed Smut

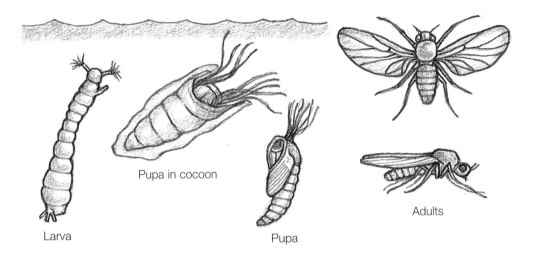

Larva

Pupa in cocoon

Pupa

Adults

Hover Fly

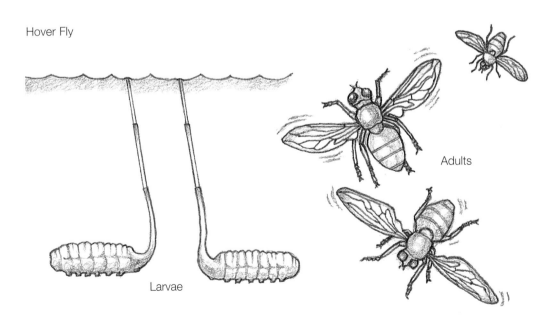

Larvae

Adults

Alder Fly
(Plate 55)

The alder fly becomes available to fish in both the larval and adult stages, the pupal stage occurring in damp ground on the riverbank. The larva has a long, segmented body with one tail; the head, which is fairly formidable, has strong jaws for feeding on smaller invertebrates. There are three pairs of legs, and running down each side of the abdomen are feathery gills. These, along with the single tail, are covered in tiny hairs. This is usually reflected in the artificial.

When the larva has reached maturity it crawls ashore and pupates in a small chamber in soft ground. The adult emerges after a few weeks and is usually to be found amongst riverside vegetation from May onwards. The alder fly is a poor flier and said to be of doubtful interest to fish. However, because of its poor flying ability, many windborne casualties must occur and at times become of interest to the hungry trout. The adult is blackish-brown and fairly stout with four glossy wings that are carried 'tent' shaped over the body when at rest. Although some patterns do exist, there are not many and a medium-sized sedge pattern of the correct colour would suffice.

Plate 55

Alder Fly

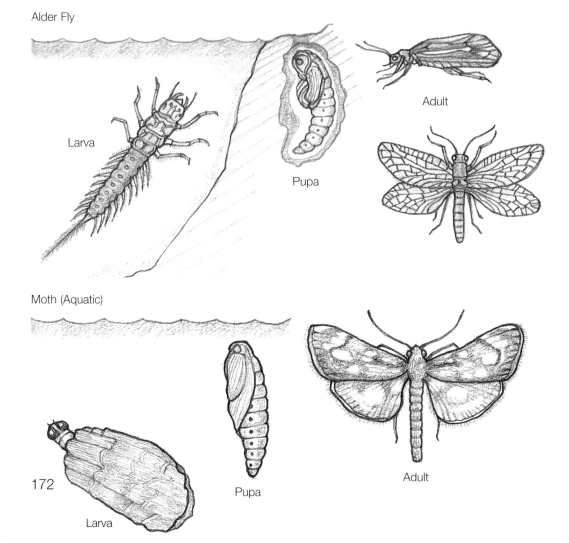

Larva

Pupa

Adult

Moth (Aquatic)

Larva

Pupa

Adult

Moths (Aquatic)
(Plate 56)

Although the larval stage of the aquatic moth is illustrated, this it is mostly for interest – as far as the flytier-fisherman is concerned this stage is of little significance. In the aquatic stage the case is made from cut pieces of leaf that are held together with silk. Sometimes this case is free-floating whilst, at other times, it is attached to plant material and therefore of little interest to a feeding fish.

The adult female lays her eggs in water and, along with some terrestrial moths, will be found flying low over the water surface on warm, moist summer evenings. At this time they become obvious to the predatory trout.

I do not need to go into the obvious shape of the adult moth and several patterns do exist to cover various colours and so on. If you were caught without a pattern, a fairly pale sedge would no doubt fill the gap.

Plate 56

Crane Fly
(Plate 56)

Also known as 'daddy-longlegs', most species of crane fly are land bred but a few have aquatic larvae. These aquatic larvae are long and grub-shaped, usually grey-white or brown in colour and carnivorous. They live in the sediment and detritus of the river or lake bed and so are not easily accessible to trout although, at times, they must be taken and patterns to represent them do exist. The artificial is simple in design but must be weighted to fish at depth.

The adult is a different matter and many artificials have been designed. Because of its large and, at times, active nature on the water surface it can be irresistible to the trout. The adult has a long, slim abdomen with a small head, pronounced thorax, long, slender wings and very long, thin legs. The overall colour is usually a shade of grey-brown. The artificial can either be fished static or 'twitched' over the water surface.

Crane Fly

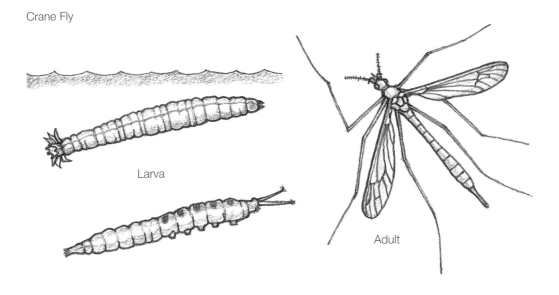

Larva

Adult

Beetles
(Plate 57)

Beetles vary in shape and size both in the larval and adult forms. The larger beetles are voracious carnivores and will attack small invertebrates, small fish and tadpoles. The dytiscus larva can grow up to 50mm and has a pair of formidable jaws for seizing its prey. At the opposite end of the spectrum is the riffle beetle larva, which is very small and shaped like an inverted teardrop. The illustration shows the basic beetle and larva shapes and there are patterns to cover most of those that grow to any size worthy of attention by the fly-tier. The colours of the larvae are usually some shade of brown, the adult forms are black or brown. The colours are considerably more varied in the land-bred beetles, which can often fall or be blown on to the water.

Plate 57

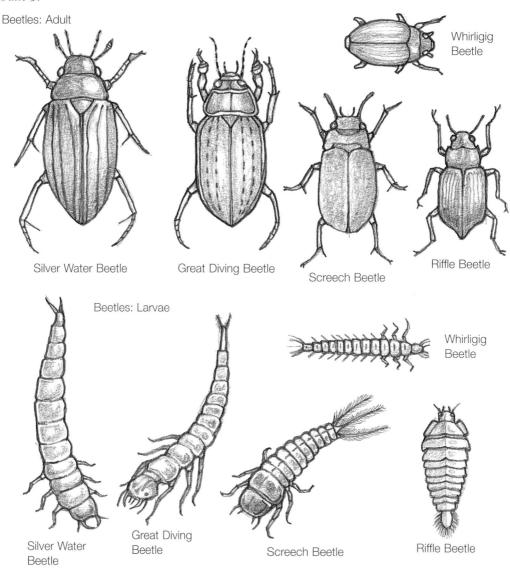

Beetles: Adult

Whirligig Beetle

Silver Water Beetle

Great Diving Beetle

Screech Beetle

Riffle Beetle

Beetles: Larvae

Whirligig Beetle

Silver Water Beetle

Great Diving Beetle

Screech Beetle

Riffle Beetle

Index